Facilitating Students' Collaborative Writing

Bruce W. Speck

ASHE-ERIC Higher Education Report: Volume 28, Number 6
Adrianna J. Kezar, Series Editor

Prepared and published by

JOSSEY-BASS
A Wiley Company
San Francisco

In cooperation with

ERIC Clearinghouse on Higher Education
The George Washington University
URL: www.eriche.org

Association for the Study
of Higher Education
URL: www.tiger.coe.missouri.edu/~ashe

Graduate School of Education and Human Development
The George Washington University
URL: www.gwu.edu

Facilitating Students' Collaborative Writing
Bruce W. Speck
ASHE-ERIC Higher Education Report: Volume 28, Number 6
Adrianna J. Kezar, Series Editor

This publication was prepared partially with funding from the Office of Educational Research and Improvement, U.S. Department of Education, under contract no. ED-99-00-0036. The opinions expressed in this report do not necessarily reflect the positions or policies of OERI or the Department.

ISSN 0884-0040   electronic ISSN 1536-0709   ISBN 0-7879-5839-5

The ASHE-ERIC Higher Education Report is part of the Jossey-Bass Higher and Adult Education Series and is published six times a year by Wiley Subscription Services, Inc., a Wiley company, at Jossey-Bass, 989 Market Street, San Francisco, California 94103-1741.

For subscription information, see the Back Issue/Subscription Order Form in the back of this journal.

Prospective authors are strongly encouraged to contact Adrianna Kezar at (301) 405-0868 or kezar@wam.umd.edu.

Visit the Jossey-Bass Web site at **www.josseybass.com.**

Printed in the United States of America on acid-free recycled paper.

Executive Summary

Collaborative writing is commonly considered as two or more persons writing together. Although this definition seems intuitively sound, it belies the fact that *all* writing is collaborative. Every writer not only uses a language that he or she inherited but also refers to the works of other writers explicitly (as when writers employ citations) or implicitly (as when writers use standard formats). Collaboration in writing is thus interwoven in the writing process in both obvious and subtle ways. *Facilitating Students' Collaborative Writing* promotes the concept that all writing is collaborative and explains that collaborative writing is a useful pedagogical tool professors can use to help students actively learn.

How Does Collaborative Writing Promote Active Learning?

Professors might cavil that learning naturally requires interaction between the student and the subject matter, and they therefore could reject the claim that collaborative writing promotes active learning. Although it is true that learning naturally requires some form of interaction, it is also true that some forms of interaction are more active and others are more passive. Lectures, for instance, tend to require students to act in ways that are more passive than the level of student involvement with learning required by collaborative writing activities. Lecturing, in general, does not promote higher-order thinking skills—synthesis, analysis, and evaluation—because lecturing, as it has traditionally been practiced, promotes the acquisition and storing of information, allowing little time in class for students to synthesize, analyze, and evaluate the material they are being given. Lecturing, as one method for helping students learn, has its place in the bag of tools professors can use to promote learning, but other methods, such as collaborative writing, promise greater potential for engaging students in active learning by drawing on the resources students themselves bring to class—their ideas, their critical facilities to ask unique questions, their ability to teach each other, their knowledge about a wide range of topics.

What Role Do Professors Play in the Collaborative Writing Classroom?

The focus of the traditional classroom tends to be the professor as the source of knowledge. In the collaborative writing classroom, however, the focus is the learning that is taking place. In the collaborative writing classroom, also called the learning-centered classroom (Stage, Muller, Kinzie, and Simmons, 1998), the professor's role changes from that of sage on the stage to expert mentor. The professor's new job is to provide opportunities for students to take responsibility for their learning as active learners (Johnson, Johnson, and Smith, 1991). Thus, the professor's new role entails establishing a classroom environment that enables students to learn actively and practice higher-order thinking skills. This monograph suggests a range of collaborative writing opportunities professors can use to help students learn, but the bulk of the monograph is a discussion of how professors can conduct a full-blown collaborative writing project.

How Can Professors Initiate Full-Blown Collaborative Writing Projects?

Full-blown collaborative writing assignments are ones that allow students to produce multiple drafts on their way to creating presentation copy, the final draft that is given a grade. Professors can enable students to produce high-quality presentation copy by leading students through the writing process, which begins with a thorough writing assignment that provides students complete instructions about what the professor requires and what choices students have. The writing assignment is crucial because it outlines requirements that will be used to evaluate presentation copy. Thus, the writing assignment provides students with the standards they can use throughout the writing process to judge their writing and their peers' writing. Judgments made throughout the writing process are formative evaluations, and such evaluations lead logically to final judgments, called summative evaluations. The same standards are used for both formative and summative evaluations, and those standards should be clearly delineated in the writing assignment. The writing assignment is just one example of planning necessary to ensure that collaborative writing projects are successful (Flower, Wallace, Norris, and Burnett, 1994).

How Can Professors Implement a Full-Blown Collaborative Writing Project?

Professors have three major responsibilities concerning the implementation of collaborative writing projects—forming groups, training students to be effective collaborators, and managing collaborative groups. Professors can form groups by considering issues related to group size, gender, cultural differences, writing ability, and other criteria. Once groups are formed, professors need to train students to be effective collaborators by addressing issues related to group leadership, conflict resolution, and work ethic. The professor is the central authority in the classroom, but the professor can promote active learning by delegating authority to students so that they learn to take responsibility for their learning. Determining leadership within the groups is one way the professor can delegate authority, and knowing about the ways different types of groups operate can be useful in making decisions about leadership and intervening in the groups (George, 1984). In addition, professors should help students cope with task, relationship, and process conflict (Jehn, 1997) so that relationship and process conflict do not hinder the group from dealing successfully with task conflict. Professors can use techniques for dealing successfully with intragroup conflict and can address issues related to work ethic by using the *3 Be's of Collaborative Writing*. In implementing collaborative writing projects, the professor also needs to show students the relationship between behavior and evaluative criteria so that students focus their energies on task conflict, not relationship and process conflict. As the groups use the writing process to create presentation copy, professors can show students how to evaluate writing by modeling effective writing critiques and by providing structured opportunities for students to serve as peer critiquers. Because computer technology is so pervasive in higher education, professors also will want to consider ways they might use computer technology to promote collaborative writing. Finally, professors will want to consider issues related to summative evaluation. How can professors grade fairly? What about the nagging problem that collaborative writing promotes an imbalance in the work among group members and thus distorts summative evaluation? This monograph addresses these and other questions about grading, including the use of a rubric to make grading standards explicit.

Contents

Foreword

Interdisciplinary teaching, multidisciplinary research, collaborative learning, administrative learning teams: every aspect of campus life is becoming more focused on ways individuals can work together to improve the teaching and learning environment. These changes are part of a larger alteration in our national and international fabric. Corporations, industry, and individuals across professions are aware that working together develops better solutions to complex problems. And people now recognize the interdependence among individuals throughout the world, which has changed views about the need to work with others to accomplish mutual goals. The Internet and World Wide Web have made this interconnection real and visible for people.

The academy is slowly recognizing the power of collaboration over individualism as well as the necessity to change paradigms within today's context. Some academics are leading the charge to develop cross-disciplinary programs and departments, to teach in learning communities, and to focus on group projects rather than individual learning. The individualistic culture of the academy is often not friendly to calls for working in groups, shared goals, multidisciplinary teaching, or cross-divisional work. Yet collaboration has continued to be a major part of campus discussions. The movements have included service-learning, K–16 partnerships, collaborative and cooperative learning, industry partnerships, and community-college partnerships. A recurring concern is that students will not learn collaboration unless we ask them to practice it across all aspects of their academic life, including writing.

Bruce Speck's monograph is a key text in providing guidance in an area of collaboration that few people have broached. Speck, vice president for academic affairs at Austin Peay State University and previous author for the Series (*Grading Students' Classroom Writing: Issues and Strategies*), summarizes the research and provides practical advice on how to structure collaborative writing for students in the classroom. The monograph begins with compelling pedagogical support for collaborative writing projects based on the research that has emerged in cognitive and learning theory over the last thirty years. This argument is followed by helpful advice related to the range of collaborative writing opportunities that can be offered, ways to construct assignments and guide the process, ways to form groups, and approaches to integrate technology. Last, Speck returns to a topic he has written about previously—grading— that is particularly vexing for collaborative writing projects. It is often difficult topics like grading or technology that are omitted from discussions of the new pedagogies. Speck acknowledges the difficulty of using a new approach, especially because most faculty were trained in individualistic paradigms and cannot easily conceive of ways to have students work together to construct a written assignment. This monograph, however, provides the detailed support to help any faculty member, familiar with collaborative learning theory or not, to alter his or her classroom habits.

Collaboration is a necessity in our society and world. Students need to consistently see that collaboration is part of their work and learning. Writing is perhaps one of the last areas untouched by the move to work together; this monograph can help us move behind that oversight in our teaching and learning.

Adrianna J. Kezar
ASHE-ERIC Series Editor
University of Maryland

Acknowledgments

I appreciate the helpful comments from anonymous reviewers and the comments my daughter Heidi provided. In addition, my wife Carmen read the manuscript several times and unfailingly provided me with observations that spurred me on to revise my writing to make it more readable. Adrianna Kezar also has been immensely helpful in providing me with professional advice about how to shape the manuscript for publication, including reading a first draft and providing valuable suggestions. I owe a great debt of gratitude to all these collaborators for the help they extended to me, and I willingly thank them publicly for their assistance.

Pedagogical Support for Classroom Collaborative Writing Assignments

A LTHOUGH COLLABORATIVE WRITING is notoriously difficult to define, I take the position that writing is collaborative by nature, and I begin this chapter by providing evidence to support my contention. Next, I situate collaborative writing in pedagogical theory, stressing the need to promote active learning and explaining why the lecture method, as generally practiced, fails to promote active learning. The infusion of collaborative writing activities in lectures can improve students' active learning; however, active learning requires more than simply using collaborative writing to enhance lectures. Then I address challenges professors most likely will encounter when they choose to use collaborative writing in their classrooms. I note that those challenges raise issues about the role of the professor in the classroom, so I explain how the traditional role of the professor as sage-on-the-stage changes in the classroom that employs active learning, the classroom that is learning centered. Finally, I suggest practical reasons professors may want to consider for employing collaborative writing in their classrooms.

The Collaborative Nature of Writing

Intuitively, collaborative writing might appear to be quite simply a piece of writing written by more than one author. This intuitive perception frames collaborative writing in terms of attribution of authorship, suggesting that a work attributed to a single author is not collaborative. Yet if we were to ask an author, say a novelist, whether the novel he or she had written was solely his or her work, the novelist might pause before answering, realizing that the novelist's craft of writing can be traced to conversations he or she had with others, books the novelist had read about writing, various novels the novelist had read, and teachers who had influenced the novelist's writing. Probably, the novelist also would consider the variegated experiences that make up his or her life, seeing that particular interactions, even seemingly serendipitous interactions, had played a part in the novelist's thinking and writing. Begrudgingly, perhaps, the novelist might have a fleeting memory of advice editors provided for various drafts of the novel. After considering these things, the novelist might ask a counter question, "What do you mean by *collaborative writing?*"

I have begun by referring to what is commonly called *creative writing* because many people believe not only that creative writing is motivated by inspiration but also that it is produced out of the author's genius. Creative writers, so the myth goes, are just gifted writers. To suggest that a literary author collaborated with anyone is, for some, to engage in heretical statements. But the fact is that *all* authors collaborate in multiple ways when they write. And literary collaboration, particularly two or more authors working together to produce a piece of fiction or poetry, is no secret to the literature on collaborative writing (Bendixen, 1986; Bishop, 1995; Bonetti, 1988; Brady, 1994; Brooker, 1994; Brown, 1985; Field, 1987; Griffin, 1987; Guyer and Petry, 1991; Haws and Engel, 1987; Inge, 1994; Knox-Quinn, 1990; Laumer, 1977; Pennisi and Lawler, 1994; Stillinger, 1991; Watson-Roulin and Peck, 1985; Yagelski, 1994).

I suggested some of the ways literary authors could collaborate when I speculated about what might run through the novelist's mind when asked about collaborative writing. Those ways of collaborating, however, are not limited to literary authors; they are typical of all writing. That is, authors of many different kinds of documents call upon experiences that have shaped their ability to write, consult models of the genre in which they are working (other novels for novelists, other business reports for writers of business reports), and seek input from audiences during the writing process. (See Figure 1 for a model of the writing process.) Elsewhere, I have noted that the normal writing process is not clean and linear (Speck, 2000, pp. 1–2), and here I affirm that the production of "finished" text is a recursive process with blind alleys and potholes, making revision an inescapable reality. In fact, a common saying among those who have studied writing theory is that "writing is revising" (Murray, 1991), or as Zinsser (1988) says, "the essence of writing is rewriting" (p. 15). The well-documented existence of the writing process (e.g., Elbow, 1981; Flower and Hayes, 1981; Murray, 1991) should help dispel the myth of inspiration as the font of text production, and it follows that writers do not write in a vacuum of creativity. In fact, they create given the primary tool that has been passed to them: language. And that tool is the product of many efforts.

Our Collaboration with Language

We inherit the language with which we write, and the language we inherit is a product of many influences, some traceable, some not traceable. We may coin new phrases, invent new spellings, create new words, and establish a particular style of writing connected with our names (such as Addisonian sentences), but we

The production of "finished" text is a recursive process with blind alleys and potholes, making revision an inescapable reality.

inherit the language that enables us to do any of these things. We may build on the work of others who have had a hand in building the language (or neglect their work or seek to tear it down), but we cannot deny that we collaborate with them in our use of the language. For most of us, this collaboration, this free use of their ideas and even the way the ideas have been shaped, is unconscious.

This unconscious collaboration with language begins when we learn to speak by listening to the way we hear our parents and friends speak, and because speaking is so natural, we may never stop to question our facility with the spoken language. When we write, we may begin to transcribe our speech, until we find that writing is not exactly speaking. As Sperling (1996) reminds us, "Because virtually everyone learns to speak fluently while only some people learn to write well, writing's relationship to speaking is especially compelling for educators to ponder" (p. 53). As writers, we know something about the complex relationship between writing and speaking as we try to find out how to write. In trying to find out how to write, we are influenced by our teachers, whether for good or ill, as they provide us with rules, guidelines, models, and opinions about what constitutes "good" writing. Little do we realize that

FIGURE 1
A Model of the Writing Process

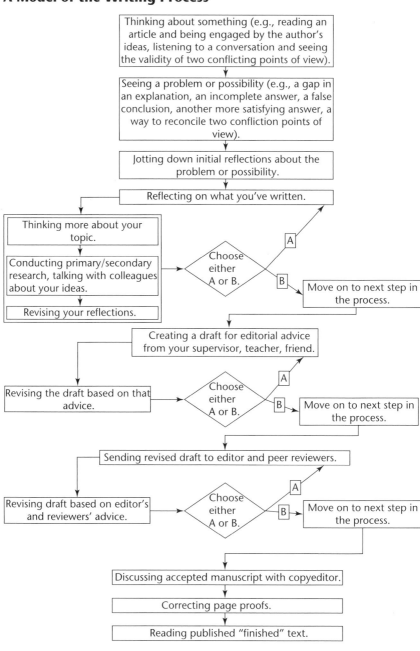

when we are asked to write something as mundane as the essay about "my summer vacation" that we are working in a particular genre with particular expectations. We write a lab report in our high school chemistry class and enter into the wonders of passive voice and the mysteries of scientific discourse with features that can be traced to Francis Bacon (Aughterson, 2000). And in all these writing experiences—even the personal diary, a genre that has a long history (Autrey, 1987)—we are collaborating with others who have shaped the genre we use, with those who have added and subtracted from the language we employ to express ourselves. In ways that we cannot escape, when we write we collaborate with many unseen people in our culture, past and present. (In fact, we collaborate with people from Western culture because our English has been greatly influenced by borrowings from Latin and Greek.) As Elsbree (1985) affirms, "At its best, composition is a corporate activity involving fellow readers, writers, and teachers. Sharing views, experiences, or research with others and submitting them for criticism, discussion, and modification are essential parts of the process of effective communication" (pp. 23–24). Collaboration in writing, then, is the norm. The real fiction is the attribution of single authorship to any work of writing, a fiction that is belied by the various written acknowledgments authors customarily make to those who have helped them: colleagues, peer reviewers, editors, esteemed mentors, parents, spouses, and children.

I am not saying that writing cannot be a solitary act in which a person sits before a computer monitor and creates text that has not been created before. Much writing gets done exactly that way. Rather, I am saying that whatever text this solitary figure produces is indebted to other texts produced by other writers, some working alone, some working together. The word some people use to talk about this interreliance of text is *intertextuality* (Porter, 1986). Not only, then, is it true that no writer writes alone but also that no text exists alone. Texts depend upon other texts. Professors know the truth of this statement, and they can demonstrate it easily by pointing to a piece of research writing, which cites sources. In academic writing, to argue a point without reference to the work of others who have also addressed the same point is rare. This long-standing tradition of collaboration is kept alive by the perennial research paper so much a part of freshman composition. A major purpose of teaching freshmen how to write a research paper is that such a paper will be the stock-in-trade of their academic experience. In fact, is it not the case that when professors write professionally they write within academic traditions and are required to satisfy standards of writing they have not created, standards that have developed over time through the work of many minds? In other words, our own efforts to write confirm the truth that writing is collaborative, and our own efforts to write give us some insights into the truth that no writer writes alone. Clearly, writing is inherently collaborative—whether academic or "creative"—and the interreliance of a text on other texts, the intertextuality of texts, is one major piece of evidence that supports the inherent collaborative nature of writing.

A person could retort to what I have said by questioning the relationship between text production and authorial attribution: "Well, I see your point about the 'collaborative' nature of writing, but I don't see why single authorship is so bad. Do you recommend putting everybody's name on a book cover or article, from Francis Bacon to the person who actually wrote a scientific research article?" Attribution of authorship, whether single or multiple, is a useful fiction for a variety of reasons, and virtually any writer would have difficulty tracing the various influences on his or her writing so as to provide attribution for everyone who had a hand in helping create a piece of writing. So I am not advocating a radical change in the way that we attribute authorship. Rather, I am suggesting that the fiction of authorial attribution hides from us important truths about how text is produced, and we should not confuse attribution with text production. Therefore, we should not assume that authorial attribution is an adequate basis for explaining text production. Ghost writing, for example, thoroughly confuses attribution with text production, and such confusion can be a cause for concern in scientific discourse (Sharp, 2000).

The Responsibility of All Professors to Teach Writing
That writing is inherently collaborative appears to be a good reason to rethink how writing is used in the classroom. When professors consider the various ways texts are really produced, they also should consider how they can integrate text production processes in the writing they ask their students to do. It really makes little sense to take the fiction of author attribution and build a

pedagogy of writing on that fiction. Does it not make better sense to use writing in our classrooms to mirror the ways texts are produced, not only in academic but also nonacademic settings, than to confuse the fiction of authorial attribution with the way writing gets done?

To incorporate writing in the classroom without understanding its collaborative nature is to teach incorrectly, perhaps even incompetently. When I talk about competence in teaching writing, I have in mind all faculty, not just those faculty who have particular credentials in teaching writing. Although colleges and universities hire professors with a specialization in writing to teach courses such as freshman composition, advanced composition, business writing, technical writing, creative writing, and so on, the teaching of writing is the responsibility of the entire faculty. Why? Because writing is not like other subjects. In declaring that English teachers should not be given the sole responsibility for teaching writing, Zinsser (1988) says that English teachers "shouldn't have to assume the whole responsibility for imparting a skill that's basic to every area of life. That should be everybody's job. That's citizenship" (p. 13). Writing, just like speaking, applies to all the content areas (Fulwiler, 1986; Fulwiler, Gorman, and Gorman, 1986; McLeod and Maimon, 2000; Stanley and Ambron, 1991).

To incorporate writing in the classroom without understanding its collaborative nature is to teach incorrectly, perhaps even incompetently.

A professor of composition does not need to know anything about nuclear physics to teach writing, but a professor of nuclear physics needs to know about writing pedagogy to teach students how to write in the nuclear physics class. In fact, the professor of composition, in virtually all cases, cannot provide adequate insight for students to produce acceptable writing in nuclear physics, particularly when writing assignments call upon students to use the form, language, and style unique to scientific writing in general and the writing of nuclear physicists in particular. The professor of composition can collaborate with professors throughout the curriculum by providing students with foundational principles of writing, including extensive practice in the writing process, but such collaboration is reciprocal. Professors throughout the curriculum have an obligation to reinforce the writing pedagogy based on the process approach that has been introduced in freshman composition. To be an agent of reinforcement, professors throughout the curriculum need to understand the collaborative nature of writing and to use the writing process in their classrooms. Indeed, professors very likely will want to understand why collaborative writing is such a powerful pedagogical tool, so now I explain how collaborative writing is situated in pedagogical theory.

Collaborative Writing and Pedagogical Theory

The umbrella term for pedagogical collaboration is *cooperative learning,* defined as "the instructional use of small groups so that students work together to maximize their own and each other's learning" (Johnson, Johnson, and Smith, 1991, p. 12). However, simply putting students in groups and asking them to work together does not fulfill the conditions necessary for cooperative learning. In fact, Johnson, Johnson, and Smith (1991) discuss five essential components of cooperative learning: "To be cooperative, a group must have clear positive interdependence and members must promote each other's learning and success face to face, hold each other individually accountable to do his or her fair share of the work, appropriately use the interpersonal and small-group skills needed for cooperative efforts to be successful, and process as a group how effectively members are working together" (p. 25).

Cooperative learning focuses on students' taking responsibility for their learning by being given classroom opportunities to have authority in learning. That is, the classroom is pedagogically constructed so that students make choices about their learning and are seen as coworkers who bring talents to the classroom that need to be used for everyone to learn. In fact, professors also are collaborators in the classroom. Thus, "students and faculty can learn from each other" (Matthews, 1996, p. 104). One implication of this mutual learning is that, as Fosnot (1991) says, "Learning needs to be conceived as something a learner does, not something that is done *to* a learner" (p. 5). Collaborative writing fits nicely with the premises that support cooperative learning and logically shares the pedagogical presuppositions of active learning.

In fact, literature on learning theory asserts that promoting students' responsibility for their learning and enabling students to develop critical skills are based on the supposition that learning is interactive (e.g., Fosnot, 1991; Perkins, 1999). Professors might shake their heads in wonder at such a statement, thinking, "Of course learning is interactive! How could it not be?" The real issue is *how* interactive is learning? If a person reads a book, there is some level of interaction, depending in part on the motivation of the person reading the book, the level of difficulty of the book's content for the person, and the prior knowledge the person brings to the reading of the book. For instance, a student might be motivated to study biology but upon reading a chapter in a biology textbook become frustrated because the student's prior knowledge of biology is not sufficient to adequately process the chapter's content. The student might learn more, however, by participating in a lab exercise that covers essentially the same material in the chapter that was so hard to process. Both reading a book and participating in a lab exercise are interactive ways of learning, but the lab exercise is more interactive because the student is involved in a hands-on environment. The student is expected to bring more of his or her senses to bear on the task at hand.

Engaging students' senses in learning is what Bonwell and Eison (1991) affirm when they define active learning as "anything that 'involves students in doing things and thinking about the things they are doing'" (p. 2). Chickering and Gamson (1987), in their widely published "Seven Principles for Good Practice" for teaching, also stress the importance of active learning. "Learning is not a spectator sport. Students do not learn much just by sitting in class listening to teachers, memorizing prepackaged assignments, and spitting out answers. They must talk about what they are learning, write about it, relate it to past experiences, apply it to their daily lives. They must make what they learn part of themselves" (p. 3). Active learning is so much a part of effective teaching that Ericksen (1984) states, "When the class hour is ended, good teachers have weakened, if not cut, the instructional dependencies of their students by leading them to exercise, independently, their continuous pursuit of knowledge within a framework of values" (p. 11). Issler (1983) says as much when he notes, "True teaching should reflect a view of the student as capable of critical thinking and self-direction . . . " (p. 341). Excellent teaching, it appears, fosters active learning so that students are not seen as passive vessels into which knowledge is poured but are viewed as active participants in the learning process, capable of bringing abilities and ideas to that process that will enhance their learning.

The Lecture Method and Passive Learning

The need for active learning in higher education generally comes under scrutiny when it comes face to face with the lecture method, the most widely used method of instruction in higher education (McKeachie, 1999; O'Donnell and Dansereau, 1994). Those who defend the lecture method might point to ways in which lectures are interactive. A student may attend a class lecture, listen attentively, take notes, and even ask questions about the lecture. Clearly, the student is interacting with the material, the professor, and, perhaps in a limited way, peers in the class. But this type of interaction, according to those who promote active learning (e.g., Bonwell and Eison, 1991; Bruffee, 1987; Johnson, Johnson, and Smith, 1991; Stage, Muller, Kinzie, and Simmons, 1998), can be greatly enhanced to help students learn even more. The central problem with whatever learning that takes place during a lecture is that in many ways students are passive (Biggs, 1996). Such an evaluation may sound extraordinarily shortsighted, given the activities of listening, taking notes, and asking questions, but let us analyze the situation.

First, the student is trying to write down information from the lecture—main ideas, quotes, illustrations, dates, references to other sources, and so forth. In many ways, these activities are not much different from transcribing the professor's comments. Although there may be value to such transcribing, it really is relatively passive in terms of learning. Second, because the student is busy transcribing, he or she probably has little time to reflect on the material. In fact, reflection on the material being transcribed could be a hindrance to the transcription process. The student could miss a vital fact or explanation. O'Donnell and Dansereau (1994), in criticizing the typical lecture method because it does not allow students to encode information in long-term memory by rehearsing, reorganizing, and elaborating on the information, remark, "A typical undergraduate rarely has the opportunity to engage in these encoding processes during a lecture. When students take notes, the notes are likely to be incomplete and contain errors. Encoding of information is likely to be impoverished, and a reliance on inadequate notes for review is likely to compound students' difficulties" (p. 117). Third, even the questions the student asks are usually requests for more information or clarification of information presented. Fourth, the great advantage of the lecture method is that it is a vehicle for providing a large amount of information in a short time (Frederick, 1986), and this advantage is also its greatest weakness in terms of student learning. Students are fed a large meal, and the chef assumes that students have the capacity to digest—and appreciate—the cuisine from the chef's culinary arts. Verner and Dickinson (1967) note, however, that students' ability to retain information from lectures is quite limited.

This four-point analysis of the impact of the lecture on the student suggests that very little learning takes place in terms of higher-order thinking skills—synthesis, analysis, and evaluation. Unless the lecturer includes opportunities for students to practice those skills, such as a written one-minute summary of the lecture toward the end of class (Wilson, 1986), scripted cooperation (Dansereau, 1988; O'Donnell and Dansereau, 1992, 1994), or other active learning techniques (Cooper and Robinson, 2000; MacGregor, Cooper, Smith, and Robinson, 2000), the students have to use higher-order thinking skills on their own time. Little or no time during the class period is devoted to explicit opportunities for synthesis, analysis, and evaluation—by the students. The professor may do a wonderful job of synthesizing, analyzing, and evaluating during the lecture, but students are not given the opportunity to practice such skills. They observe an expert synthesizer, analyzer, and evaluator, but they sit—perhaps with awe, envy, amusement, puzzlement, or disgust—and observe. The curious assumption seems to be that by watching someone do something a person can become an expert in that same something. This is exactly Huber's (1992) contention when he points out the fallacy, accepted widely in the academy, that the way to train students to be good teachers is to have them watch good teachers teach. "Teachers are apparently supposed to know how to teach because they have been watching teachers do it since first grade—kind of like learning how to play tennis by sitting in a grandstand" (p. 124). The lecture method suffers from the same shaky assumption about the relationship between seeing and doing.

I am not saying that the lecture method should be abolished. I am saying that it can—and should—be changed to include more active learning. I also am saying that the lecture method is not the best model for active learning because lectures tend not to foster higher-order thinking and conceptual understanding (Saroyan, 2000). The best models for active learning put the responsibility for synthesis, analysis, and evaluation on the students' shoulders by structuring classrooms so that students have the most opportunities for taking responsibility for using higher-order thinking skills. Students in such classrooms are called upon to apply their skills to solve problems.

Although various methods can be used to support active learning, I assert that collaborative writing is a highly valuable method because students have to be active in writing. I am not saying, of course, that the very act of writing requires active learning. Professors have read student writing that for all intents and purposes lacks evidence of much cerebral activity, merely testifying to the physical act of transcription, so when I speak of writing, I am not talking about the mere act of transcription; rather, I am talking about writing as a thinking process, writing as a method of learning actively. In referring to writing as a method of active learning, I am focusing on writing to learn as a prelude to writing to inform (Speck, 2000, pp. 11–14). That is, students need to use writing as a tool to figure out what they want to say *before* they formalize their thoughts to inform others about what the students have learned from their writing.

Learning-Centered Classrooms

Unlike the lecture, the classroom based on a highly interactive model of student learning metaphorically puts students at the center of the classroom; the professor is still very important to the classroom but acts now as a manager, mentor, coach. Such classrooms are called student-centered classrooms, but I prefer to call them *learning-centered classrooms,* because the focus is not on students but on learning. For instance, in learning-centered classrooms, students have the authority and responsibility to make decisions about what to read, to select topics within the framework of the class that interest them, to work on collaborative projects with written and oral components. Thus, students consult with various authorities, including various kinds of texts (government documents, Internet articles, information from Web sites, books, pamphlets, interviews, and so on), and have an expert consultant—the professor—to help them learn more about how to learn. Students also consult with each other, tap into each other's knowledge bases, and learn to work as a team. A large part of interactive learning includes interaction among students so that they can profit from each other's insights. Thus, learning is well served by student-student interaction in complex problem-solving projects, precisely the kind of projects that are possible through collaborative writing assignments.

When professors create classrooms where students work with other students, the professors should assume that students have something to bring to the knowledge table. They are not blank slates upon which knowledge is transcribed or vessels waiting to be filled with knowledge. Certainly, students still need to learn facts and philosophical viewpoints, but the purpose of learning facts and others' philosophical viewpoints is to provide students with tools to think critically. The application of these tools, their use in the exercise of critical thinking, must extend to applications in the world, to the enacting of the results of critical thinking. In fact, without such applications, critical thinking itself becomes a sterile exercise. Learning, then, is inseparably linked with doing.

Professors might object to learning-centered classrooms by noting that very often when students are put in groups in the classroom they simply "share their ignorance" or, more likely, their social experiences the night before the class and their social expectations for the weekend. Two points can be made about such a qualm. First, group members sharing ignorance is not unique to students. Departmental meetings, committee meetings, and faculty senate meetings do not entirely escape the charge of a body of people sharing their ignorance. Yet out of such sharing, misconceptions can be addressed, issues raised, new initiatives suggested. Second, the way in which groups approach a task has a great deal to do with the efficacy of whatever sharing takes place. Thus, the chapter in this monograph devoted to teaching students how to be effective collaborators ("Forming Groups") includes suggestions for ways the professor can manage collaborative groups effectively. If collaborative writing groups degenerate into merely "sharing ignorance," something is amiss in the classroom; however, professors have at their disposal a variety of strategies for ensuring that collaborative writing groups have the optimal opportunity for success.

Learning-centered classrooms also have the great advantage of creating a community of learners, a community of people who can support each other and learn from each other. As participants in a community of learners, students have the opportunity not only to share their knowledge with other students and to learn from their peers but also to hear how other students as members of a live audience respond to their writing. In fact, audience is one of the two focal points for discussing writing pedagogy, the other point being purpose. Professors have a responsibility to explain to students how to write for particular purposes and for particular audiences. Fortunately, a classroom offers a ready-made audience for writing, and professors can train and employ the members of this audience as critiquers of their peers' writing. As critiquers of peers' writing, students learn principles of effective writing for a particular discipline and can use those skills to analyze their own writing. In making the claim that collaborative writing is a premier method of learning, I am not saying that when professors accept the truth about the efficacy of collaborative writing and see the need to revise their teaching pedagogy, they will enter nirvana. Quite the contrary.

Challenges to Integrating Collaborative Writing in the Classroom

If professors see the value of collaborative writing and choose to use collaborative writing assignments in their classrooms, they will encounter challenges, the same challenges that are associated with collaborative pedagogies. For instance, one of the major costs of using collaborative writing is time. Learning how to implement the writing process in the classroom takes time. Implementing the writing process in the classroom takes time. Evaluating students' writing using a healthy dose of both formative and summative evaluation takes time. In some cases, the design of the course will need to be altered, which is a time-consuming process. I have no easy answers to the time problem. Teaching students how to write takes time, and I see no quick way to help students practice the writing process in their classes and engage in significant collaborative writing opportunities without using class time, sometimes significant amounts of class time.

Another challenge to using collaborative writing in the classroom that compounds the challenge of how to use classroom time is the relationship between inculcating course content and helping students to think critically (as a person would think critically in a particular discipline). In the various writing-across-the-curriculum workshops that I have conducted, invariably the following question is asked: How can professors take time away from teaching content, especially when there is so much content to cover in one semester, to promote the writing process? Again, I have no easy answer to that question. But professorial concerns about content coverage strike at the heart of debates about collaborative writing pedagogy, because those concerns raise issues about the nature of teaching and learning. If learning is interactive, however, then the best classroom pedagogies incorporate healthy doses of interaction in the curriculum, including opportunities for students to engage in collaborative writing.

Allied with concerns about time and content coverage is the challenge of student-professor discontent. Collaborative writing can make both professor and students uneasy because collaborative writing pedagogy asks them to investigate their assumptions about teaching and learning. In investigating those assumptions, professors and students may experience anxiety, and students may resent—at least at first—the departure from what they have come to see as traditional patterns of student-student and student-professor behaviors. Felder and Brent (1996) accurately describe the uneasiness that generally accompanies the introduction of active learning in the classroom: "Student-centered instruction may impose steep learning curves on everyone involved. The teacher feeling awkward and the students hostile are both common and natural" (p. 43). Reinforcing the legitimacy of collaborative writing in classroom pedagogy takes on a new urgency when we admit that using collaborative writing in the classroom is necessary and may cause students and professors discomfort when it is introduced in the classroom.

Generally, the challenges I have cited bring into focus a tension between two very different assumptions about what constitutes effective teaching and learning. Professorial concerns about the use of classroom time, content coverage, and disruption of student-professor relationships are grounded in a pedagogy that promotes the lecture method and, concomitantly, what has been labeled *passive learning*. Collaborative writing pedagogy, however, is grounded in a pedagogy that promotes the learning-centered classroom and active learning. Ultimately, professors align themselves with either a pedagogy that stresses passive learning or a pedagogy that stresses active learning—which is not to say that professors have to abandon the lecture method but that philosophically professors will adhere either to a pedagogy based on the premises that undergird active learning or to a pedagogy based on the premises that undergird passive learning. Whichever pedagogical perspective a professor takes has significant implications for the ways the professor structures the classroom, balances concerns about content coverage and critical thinking, and frames the nature of learners. In fact, the professor who embraces a collaborative writing pedagogy may have to reconsider his or her role in the classroom. Indeed, the professorial role in the classroom may have to be revised when professors use collaborative writing to help students learn.

The Role of the Professor in Classroom Collaborative Writing Assignments

When students work as collaborators, the role of the professor is changed, because the professor is seen neither as the sole authority in the classroom nor the physical focal point of the classroom. Students take on a new role as active learners, and professors, by necessity, take on a new role as expert mentors because "collaboration and mentoring are often closely intertwined" (Jipson and Paley, 2000, p. 37). This change in professorial role can be a major issue for professors accustomed to the traditional model of the professor as lecturer.

When students work as collaborators, the role of the professor is changed.

Many, if not most, of the teachers professors sat under in graduate school organized their classrooms around the lecture method, sometimes called the sage-on-the-stage model. As Davis (1993) points out, "For hundreds of years, college teaching was typified by a professor reading a lecture to an audience of note-taking students. The professor's duties were to compose and present authoritative lectures, to test students on their knowledge and to assign grades" (p. xix). In fact, the literature on effective teaching includes numerous examples of exceptional professors who were noted for their ability to lecture well (e.g., Baiocco and DeWaters, 1998; Epstein, 1981). Unsurprisingly, the lecture method continues to be the ruling paradigm for teaching in higher education (McKeachie, 1999; O'Donnell and Dansereau, 1994).

The focal point of the lecture method is the lecturer, who, when things go well, really does emulate the sage on the stage. Good lecturers, it seems, provide lots of wise insights in an entertaining, engaging way. Professors who have become comfortable with the sage-on-the-stage model may not quite know what their role should be when the classroom is changed to include collaborative writing. In fact, they may be uncomfortable integrating the role of collaborative writing mentor into their role as expert lecturer. To assuage possible concerns about the new responsibilities professors need to assume if they intend to use collaborative writing effectively, I affirm that professors' use of collaborative writing in their classrooms does not mean that professors have to denounce the lecture method and forsake every other pedagogical tool they have developed for the sake of engaging students in collaborative writing. As I will show in a moment, collaborative writing can be integrated into classrooms in various ways, some small, some large. Therefore, I agree with Hutchings (1996) when she says that the focus of the classroom should be learning, not method: "Putting the emphasis on learning mitigates otherwise divisive debates about the 'best' teaching methods, where the advocates of, say, cooperative learning line up on one side of the room and the devotees of lecture on the other, pointing fingers at each other. Shifting attention from how teachers teach to what (and how well) our students learn makes for more constructive debate and problem solving" (p. 37). Collaborative writing is one method professors can use to help students learn. As Dale (1997) observes, when a professor engages students in collaborative writing, he or she "becomes a facilitator of learning rather than a transmitter of knowledge" (p. 17). But professors do need to have some understanding of what their responsibilities are as facilitators of learning in classroom collaborative writing opportunities. Obviously, professors cannot lecture while students are working and writing collaboratively. So what role does the professor play?

The following chapters explain many parts of the role that professors play in collaborative writing projects: creator of writing assignments, trainer of groups, manager of the collaborative process, evaluator of students' efforts. So I do not deal with those critical and necessary parts of the professor's role now. Rather, I focus on the overarching role of mentor as it relates to collaborative writing in the classroom.

In focusing on the overarching role of mentor, I could be misunderstood as saying that unless professors are engaging their students in collaborative writing projects they are not being mentors who seek to help students grow intellectually. I do not espouse that position. Rather, I espouse the position that collaborative writing adds an additional challenge to the professor's role as a mentor who seeks to help students write effectively. No longer only the sage on the stage, the professor now has opportunities to work with students individually and in groups, to model particular behaviors he or she expects of students, to change the dynamics of the classroom. No longer is the professor in the position of giving only a scripted commentary on a topic. Now the professor has to deal with issues that arise spontaneously and that may not have one set answer. The new role, therefore, asks of professors that they trust the process of collaborative writing, even when it appears to be quite messy and chaotic. (See Figure 2 for a model of the collaborative writing process.)

Trusting the process does not mean that professors throw themselves at the mercy of the collaborative writing process. Instead, it means that professors accept the high probability that when they structure collaborative writing assignments wisely, according to the research findings and classroom experiences of those who have gone before them, they will have every reason to believe that collaborative writing tasks can be successful. So my first recommendation for assuming the new professorial role as collaborative writing mentor is for professors to continue gaining insight into the theory and practice

FIGURE 2
A Model of the Collaborative Writing Process

A decision is made to form a group (e.g., supervisor ascertains that a project will require a group effort, two or more researchers determine to work together to solve a problem, professor devises an assignment to help students write collaboratively).

↓

Groups are formed and either given the responsibility to divide the labor or assigned tasks by the supervisor or professor. Self-formed groups determine how labor will be divided.

↓

Group members confer and seek classification of assignment/task, discuss roles of group members, and establish timetable and milestones.

↓

Group members work individually and in various subgroups to prepare drafts of assigned/selected sections of the assignment. See Figure 1 for the initial steps in the writing process group members will use to create drafts.

↓

Group members read and comment on drafts from subgroups. Based on these comments, a subgroup will revise its draft. This process of comment and revise will continue until the group puts the entire document together. See Figure 1 for recursive steps in revising process.

↓

Group assembles efforts of subgroups to create the first iteration of the master draft. Issues related to stylistic consistency, redundancy, logic, and organization are primary considerations.

↓

Group continues to refine master draft, ultimately treating issues related to grammar, mechanics, spelling, pagination, numbering of graphics, and so forth.

↓

Master draft undergoes internal review (e.g., editorial review by a company editor, in-class review by another group).

↓

Group revises based on editorial review and packages "final" version of master draft.

↓

Master draft delivered to supervisor, client, or professor.

↓

Master draft may undergo further revision based on comments by supervisor, client, or professor.

of collaborative writing, as they are doing by reading this volume, and to consult references I have cited that interest them. Having a good foundation for using collaborative writing will help professors to trust the process.

Next, professors, in trusting the process, will find that they will be called upon to work much more closely with students individually and in groups. When students are working in groups during the class, the professor may want to sit in on each group and listen to what is happening. Doing so helps the professor know what kinds of problems and successes students are encountering, and the professor may want to call all groups' attention to those problems and successes because others may be struggling with the same problems and wondering whether what they did is successful. In short, professors will want to be available to students, should they have questions during class time when collaborative writing assignments are used, and professors will want to initiate some interaction with students during the classroom collaborative writing activities. The following chapters provide insights into ways professors can interact with students successfully.

Practical Benefits of Using Collaborative Writing in the Classroom

"OK," a professor might say, "I see that collaborative writing promotes what you call active learning, and I can see that I will have to change some of my classroom practices to use collaborative writing assignments, but are there any practical benefits to using collaborative writing assignments in my classroom?" Part of the answer to that question confirms the unity of theory and practice. If collaborative writing pedagogy is cogent, professors who use collaborative writing effectively can have the assurance that they are helping students learn, promoting students' responsibility for their learning, and enabling students to develop critical skills that not only apply to their own writing but also to analysis of texts and arguments in general (Dale, 1997). I see these outcomes as practical benefits of any pedagogy, and the ability to learn is a practice benefit of collaborative writing pedagogy.

Another benefit is that professors are preparing students to be successful citizens and employees (e.g., Henson and Sutliff, 1998). As Dale (1997) affirms in discussing the benefits of collaborative writing, "students learn to cooperate and negotiate, skills which are invaluable in other situations" (p. 21). Gerlach (1994) agrees, stating, "Collaborative learning environments have many advantages for students' intellectual and social development" (p. 9).

The practical answer to the question about professors' requiring students to participate in collaborative writing projects is based on the common use of collaborative writing in the world of work. Various studies of disparate workplace settings have shown that professionals—engineers, computer programmers, bankers, scientists, journalists, and others—write collaboratively to produce documents for their employers (e.g., Couture and Rymer, 1991; Cross, 1990; Dautermann, 1993; Debs, 1991; Dillon, 1993; Ede and Lunsford, 1990; Locker, 1992; Pomerenke, 1992; Spilka, 1993a, 1993b; Sullivan, 1991). Because one purpose of higher education is to prepare students to function effectively as writers in business, government, and industry, professors can help fulfill that purpose by managing students effectively as they participate in collaborative writing projects.

The argument for teaching effective disciplinary writing should not be seen as a plea to supply workers for the military-industrial complex. Although education contains skill components (e.g., the ability to use mathematical equations, apply principles of economics, write grammatically correct sentences and paragraphs), professors desire that students use such skills in the service of higher-order learning—in problem solving that will advance the greater good of society. Johnson, Johnson, and Smith (1998) note, "Cooperative learning is the heart of problem-based learning" (p. 28), and they provide ample evidence—both theoretical and empirical—to demonstrate that "a) the theories underlying cooperative learning are valid and b) cooperative learning does indeed work in college classrooms" (p. 35). Davis (1993) concurs, saying, "Students learn best when they are actively involved in the process. Researchers report that, regardless of the subject matter, students working in small groups tend to learn more of what is taught and retain it longer than when the same content is presented in other instructional formats" (p. 147). I would add that including writing in group activities enhances students' opportunities for active learning.

Conclusion

I am not arguing for the mere pragmatic value of using collaborative writing groups in the classroom. I am arguing foremost for the intellectual good of using such groups. I am arguing that we can help students be successful citizens and productive workers when they learn how to communicate and learn effectively by tapping the natural resources of the classroom. After all, those resources are quite similar to the resources in the world of work. Ultimately, I am arguing that professors have a responsibility to enable students to communicate effectively in writing, and that when students do write effectively, they can increase their own knowledge and help others to increase their store of knowledge. Additionally, students can learn how to work with people, how to compromise effectively, how to value differences. If, however, you think that I claim too much for collaborative writing, please read on.

The Range of Collaborative Writing Opportunities

THE CLAIMS I MADE at the end of the last chapter are supported by the literature on collaborative writing and cooperative learning, but those claims are not in the form of a guarantee. Merely using something called *collaborative writing* in the classroom will not guarantee that students will become more effective writers, and, indeed, this volume is intended to give all kinds of pointers on how to use collaborative writing effectively. Professors who want to see students become more effective writers will find concrete suggestions on how to go about realizing the claims in their own classrooms.

A great deal of the literature on collaborative writing is written by professors in English, particularly professors who teach writing, and the advice they give about collaborative writing projects may seem extravagant to professors in other disciplines. For instance, professors of English who teach writing may easily include in their classes what I call a full-fledged collaborative writing project, a group project that culminates in a major written product, such as a multi-page report, along with various other hefty writing projects. Professors in disciplines other than English composition, however, often have severe constraints in terms of class size, content coverage, time available for writing, and so forth. Nevertheless, professors throughout the curriculum may want to know how collaborative writing opportunities can fit into their classes without committing themselves to the full-fledged collaborative writing project. Indeed, professors throughout

> **Merely using something called *collaborative writing* in the classroom will not guarantee that students will become more effective writers.**

the curriculum may find collaborative writing projects appealing, particularly because such projects offer significant opportunities for students to grow intellectually and learn how to work with people productively.

Collaborative writing opportunities can take various forms. For instance, professors might insert a brief collaborative writing opportunity during the class that will not require follow-up, including a grade. For other opportunities, professors may ask students to begin a project in class and to spend certain times in class and outside class as a group working on the project. In the opportunities that follow, I begin with relatively simple ways to include collaborative writing in the classroom and move to more complex ways. As will become clear, the more complex ways are more complex because they use more of the simple ways or use the simple ways in a more complex way.

Brief In-class Collaborative Writing Assignments

Professors can be very inventive, so I am going to provide an example of brief in-class collaborative writing assignments, knowing that professors in particular disciplines can apply the example to their students' writing needs. The example is a beginning-of-class recap. The professor can begin the class by asking students to write a brief summary of the major points covered in the previous class. When students have had an opportunity to write an individual summary, the professor asks students to pair up, read each other's summaries, and from those summaries write one summary. Then the professor can ask a particular dyad to read its summary to the class. The professor can ask the class whether the summary says enough. If not, what is missing? The professor can ask more dyads to read until he or she feels that the summaries have provided students with a recap of the previous class. The professor can ask students to turn in the summaries and use them to register class attendance, for some sort of minimal credit, or both. A variation of this collaborative writing opportunity is the end-of-class recap, in which students follow the same procedure but prepare a summary of what they have just been studying in class.

Those interested in other examples of brief writing assignments might consult Paulson (1999), who uses a one-minute blue book quiz at the beginning of his classes to test students' knowledge of readings assigned for that day's class; his approach could be expanded to include two or more people writing a response to a question about the assigned reading. Angelo and Cross (1993) discuss a one-sentence summary (pp. 138–187), which can be adapted to collaborative groups, and the minute paper (pp. 148–153), which also can be modified for use as a brief collaborative writing assignment. Romance and Vitale's (1999) concept mapping also has potential for use as a brief writing assignment. Geske (1992) uses a three-minute thesis as a way for students to record their reactions to an issue or videotape.

Journals are another way to promote student writing, and journals can be used a number of ways to promote active learning:

> *Through journal assignments, we can encourage many different kinds of thinking: We can ask students to summarize material, formulate questions about discussions or reading assignments, relate new information to their personal lives, apply the principles of a discipline to actual cases, or explain the process by which they have arrived at a solution to a problem. In journals they can analyze, synthesize, summarize, apply, or create. In addition, journals can give students a constant means of checking their comprehension of a subject. Through daily, informal writing about new material, students can keep in touch with what they understand or do not understand. If students are asked to share their journal writing with the rest of the class, or with partners in a group, journals can also serve as excellent prompts to class discussion and as methods of peer teaching. Daily journal writing to ponder over, read aloud, or talk about keeps students actively involved in and responsible for their own learning* [Tomlinson, 1990, p. 36].

An excellent source for learning more about using journals to promote student learning is Fulwiler's *The Journal Book,* in which Fulwiler recommends that professors not only encourage students to write but also provide opportunities for students to share their writing with others: "Every time you ask students to write in class, do something active and deliberate with what they have written: have volunteers read whole entries; have everyone read one sentence to the whole class; have neighbors share one passage with each other . . . " (1987, p. 7).

Again, the potential for using brief writing assignments in the class is great, and I have provided examples of how professors can use such writing assignments to promote collaborative learning and collaborative writing. Virtually any brief writing assignment can be adapted to become a collaborative writing assignment that includes student-student interaction.

Larger Collaborative Writing Projects

Larger collaborative writing projects require more professor-student collaboration, because students will need help with their writing assignments throughout the writing process. In the brief assignments I have discussed, most of the writing does not go beyond creating a first draft. Larger collaborative writing assignments, however, require students to go through a more involved writing process. In the next chapter, I discuss the writing process more fully, so I simply note here that writing is not linear. That is, writers do not, under most circumstances, prepare a draft, tidy it up, and launch it. Rather, writers go through a recursive process to produce a "final" draft. (I emphasize *final*, because virtually every "final" draft could be improved, but time's winged chariot drives us on to other duties, so we do the best we can within the time we are given for particular writing tasks.) That recursive process can be grueling, but if professors help students plan during the early stage of text production, students will likely find that writing is less arduous than it would be without adequate planning.

Helping Students Learn How to Select an Appropriate Topic
Collaborative planning moves us into larger collaborative writing projects, because the planning process begins with the selection of topics for a writing assignment. This is a good place to comment on the value of students' selecting their own topics. Although it may not always be possible for students to select their own topics for a writing assignment, professors will find that when students write from a knowledge base about something that interests them, the writing tends to be better than if students are asked to write about a topic they know little about and do not find engaging (Murray, 1997). As Zinsser

(1988) affirms, "Motivation is crucial to writing—students will write far more willingly if they write about subjects that interest them and that they have an aptitude for" (p. 14). Roen (1989) agrees, saying that writing assignments "need to allow students to write about topics with which they are familiar and in which they have some interest" (p. 197). Certainly, students need to expand their horizons, and it is perfectly appropriate for professors to assign topics related to a content area so that students research and write about ideas that they have hitherto not encountered. But it is not appropriate to put students in a position of having to develop a knowledge base *and* write effectively about that knowledge base in short periods of time, especially when professors expect students to write extended discourses on a topic. A semester, for most students, is a short period of time. Thus, most student research papers that evolve over a semester are disappointing. From my experience, most suffer from lack of research, i.e., an adequate knowledge base. Add to that the additional burden of students' struggling to write in a genre that is relatively unfamiliar to them. (The research papers they did in high school generally pale in comparison to the research papers they are required to do at the university.) This burden can be lightened when students are given the opportunity to investigate issues that interest them within the domain of a general topic in the content area.

For instance, a professor teaching American history might require students to write a collaborative paper on some aspect of the Civil War. Would it not be appropriate for students interested in clothing to write about uniforms, the materials that were used to construct uniforms, the insignia worn on the uniforms? For students interested in weapons, would it not be appropriate for them to write about the types of rifles used in the Civil War? (It may be that the types of rifles used in the Civil War is too large a topic for one medium-size paper, and the professor would want to help students narrow the topic to the two or three prominent types of rifles used.) In other words, I recommend that professors, as much as possible, allow students to select topics that interest them. When I have given students the freedom to choose topics, I have found that the writing is more engaging, longer, and filled with more detail than the writing that students do when they are assigned topics with which they are faintly familiar.

When the professor chooses to give students the freedom to select topics, he or she can begin helping students understand how to narrow a topic by providing an example of the topic under consideration—e.g., the Civil War—and help the students brainstorm topics in class. Let's say that in leading the class in a brainstorming session, the professor writes on the board the following topics students have spontaneously suggested: food, munitions, uniforms, battles, generals, African Americans, civilians, spies, President Lincoln, and Jefferson Davis. The professor can take one of these topics—civilians—and go through the same exercise of listing subtopics the students recommend: men, women, children, political figures, ordinary citizens, newspaper editors, spies, farmers, bankers, and shipbuilders. At this point, the professor might want to say to the class that they are getting close to a manageable topic, but they need to get even closer. So the professor can select one of the subtopics—women—and go through the same exercise of listing subtopics the students recommend: mothers, daughters, women workers of various types, prostitutes, wives, women as professionals, and women as spies. "Of course," the professor might say to the class, "none of our lists is definitive. We might even want to go back and add a category to one of the topics or subtopics later. The purpose of our brainstorming is to illustrate how to narrow our search for a manageable topic." Then the professor can begin to ask what questions the class might want to ask about, say, women as spies. Questions could include the following: Were women spies? If so, who was the most famous woman spy? How were women enlisted as spies? If women were caught as spies, how were they treated? Did women dress like men when they were spying? These questions help students see that it is helpful to narrow a topic and begin asking questions about the topic. As Bean (1996) points out, the starting point for expert writers is their perception that a problem exists: "Expert writers feel an uncertainty, doubt a theory, note a piece of unexplained data, puzzle over an observation, confront a view that seems mistaken, or otherwise articulate a question or problem" (p. 30). And professors can help students get to that starting point by helping them narrow a topic so that they can ask questions about the topics.

Frankly, we are still not at the point where we can state a thesis. "Having focused on a problem, only rarely does a skilled academic writer write a thesis statement and outline before embarking on extensive exploration, conversation, correspondence with colleagues, and even, on some occasions, writing one or more drafts. A thesis statement often marks a moment of discovery and clarification—an 'aha!' experience ('So *this* is my point! Here is my argument in a nutshell!')—not a formulaic planning device at the very start of the process" (Bean, 1996, p. 30). Thus, the professor, in helping students to narrow a topic to a manageable size and to pose questions about the narrowed topic, has prepared students to explore the topic. Now students need to do some research about the role of women as spies in the Civil War. Certainly, not all students will write about this topic—maybe none will—but the process the professor has modeled for narrowing a topic is a collaborative act designed to give students a method for arriving at their own manageable topic.

Teaching Students How to Write a Proposal

The next step in planning is to conduct preliminary research about the topic, unless the students already have a knowledge base that will allow them to write about the topic. If students need to conduct preliminary research for a collaborative writing project, the professor might organize groups of students based on their interest in a particular topic and then ask each member of the group to find one piece of information about the particular topic. After students have been given time to conduct preliminary research, the professor can reconvene the groups and ask the members to pool their research.

At this point, students need to have a plan for the entire collaborative writing project, and one way to help them plan is to ask them to write a proposal in memo format—one per group—with their narrowed topic, a schedule, responsibilities of group members, and expenses. Figure 3 is an example of such a memo. Professors may be curious, wondering why students should include expenses in the memo. First, students need to know that most proposals for business, industry, and the university would be unacceptable if they did not include expenses, and professors will want to prepare students to write successful proposals, of various types, in the world of work. Second, students need to realize that their education costs much more than merely the expense of tuition and fees. Their time is worth something, generally called *opportunity costs*. If students were not in school, they could be earning money working. I have found that when students calculate all their educational costs, they have a new appreciation for the economic value of their education.

FIGURE 3
A Group Proposal for a Writing Assignment

September 10, 2001

To: Professor Laertes

From: In from the Cold (Sandra Akins, Felix Mendez, Jake Niels, Solice Rumanda)

Subject: Group Proposal for First Writing Assignment on the Civil War

TOPIC
Southern wives as spies in the Civil War. (Note: OC means the group meets out of class. IC means the group meets in class.)

SCHEDULE

Date	Event
September 3	Combine ideas gathered from research (OC)
September 7	Begin writing first draft (IC)
September 8	Continue writing first draft (OC)
September 10	Bring first draft to class for review (IC)
September 12	Discuss first draft and begin second draft (OC)
September 15	Complete second draft (OC)
September 17	Bring second draft to class for review (IC)
September 18–20	Conduct more research (OC)
September 24–28	Write third draft (OC)
October 1	Bring third draft to class for peer review (IC)
October 2–5	Revise third draft to create fourth draft (OC)
October 6	Critique fourth draft (OC)
October 8	Revise fourth draft (OC)
October 9	Edit fourth draft (OC)
October 11	Proofread fourth draft (OC)
October 12	Submit fourth draft for professor's evaluation (IC)

RESPONSIBILITIES
All members of the group will do equal amounts of writing. The rest of the group effort is broken down like this:
Sandra—word processing, light research, revising, and editing
Felix—heavy research, revising, and proofreading
Jake—light research, formatting of paper, revising, and editing
Solice—heavy research, revising, editing, and proofreading

EXPENSES

Item	Cost
Tuition (4 × $372.50)	$1,490.00
Supplies	20.00
Labor (4 × $7/hr. / 40 hrs. each)	1,120.00
Babysitting	30.00
Travel (gas)	18.00
Food (for Saturday meetings)	45.00
Computer wear and tear	12.00
TOTAL	$2,735.00

Students can bring drafts of their collaborative proposals to the class and exchange their proposals with other groups until each group has had an opportunity to read several proposals. Then the professor can ask students what they learned from reading the proposals. Were the proposals different in any ways? Were all the proposals complete? This informal peer review of proposals enables student groups to gain insights about revising their proposals before turning them in to the professor later. Literature on collaborative planning provides more details that can be useful as professors learn how to help students plan effectively to write effectively (Burnett, 1990; Flower, Wallace, Norris, and Burnett, 1994; Lewis, 1993; Meyers, 1985; Plowman, 1993). "Collaborators must, if they are to be collaborators, work together to form a shared view on not only the nature of the problem that brings them into the writing situation but also the techniques of reasoning and patterns of presentation to be used in advancing a solution" (Enos, 1993, p. 152). A critical theoretical point to remember is that collaborative planning is a powerful tool in helping students prepare to write and in actually writing, because talking and writing are linked. That is, students who have the opportunity to talk with others, including their peers, can gain insights into what they are trying to say in written form—can clarify and generate meaning—and without this benefit, their writing undoubtedly will be less effective. Collaborative planning, which includes preparing students to write by helping them plan their writing, is not limited to these initial stages of the writing process. In fact, the value of continuing oral feedback, an important feature of collaborative planning, can be perpetuated in various writing conferences.

> **Collaborative planning is a powerful tool in helping students prepare to write and in actually writing, because talking and writing are linked.**

Modeling Response in Professor-Student Writing Conference

The professor-student writing conference is one good example of oral collaboration that can have an immense benefit to students as they revise their writing (Arbur, 1977; Bowen, 1993; Carnicelli, 1980; Duke, 1975; Fassler, 1978; Harris, 1986, 1990; Rose, 1982; Tirrell, 1981). Literature about professor-student writing conferences recommends that students come to a conference prepared to read their draft of an assignment aloud to the professor, or the professor can read the draft aloud to the student. The professor can then ask the student what he or she thinks about the draft. The student may have questions for the professor; this is a good time for the student to ask those questions.

The professor also should respond to the writing as a reader, not as a grammarian or someone who is hunting for errors. Responding as a reader may be difficult because, as Lawson and Ryan (1989) note, professors approach students' writing with a "skepticism quite unlike their approach to most other texts" (p. x). Professors tend to *expect* to find problems with student writing in ways that they would not expect to find in the newspapers, magazines, and books they read. Schwegler (1991) suggests that professors tend to approach student writing as incomplete and needing corrections because "the classroom is a site of struggle between the legitimate authority of both readers and writers, their contrasting positions in the educational hierarchy, and their respective values" (p. 221). This conflict leads to what Stewart (1975) calls responding "too emphatically to the wrong things in the wrong way" in students' writing and notes, "Our students want us to respond to the essences, not the accidents, of their papers" (p. 243). Miller (1984) echoes Stewart's position, when she suggests that teachers should view "the textual status of student writing as writings-in-progress rather than as failed products" (p. 27). After all, the purpose of the professor-student conferences early in the writing process is to help students revise their work in progress, and issues related to grammar, spelling, and punctuation can be dealt with later when the student's writing is more focused. To respond as a reader, the professor might tell the student what in the writing was particularly interesting, what was confusing, where in the writing the professor, as a reader, wanted more information. One purpose of giving students such feedback is to help them ask similar questions so that they can think like readers and learn to revise for readers. One caution is in order here. The professor should not dominate the conference, either in terms of time spent talking or in terms of advice given (Bowen, 1993). The professor is responding as a reader, and as a reader, the professor should allow and enable the student to talk most of the time by responding to open-ended questions the professor asks about the student's writing or questions the professor asks about the student's concerns.

A variation of the professor-student writing conference is the professor-students writing conference. Perhaps the professor has paired students and asked them to write one paper. The professor can schedule writing conferences for the paired students and use the same method he or she used for the professor-student writing conference. Indeed, the writing conference can work for groups larger than two students.

Modeling Response in Class

Professors also can model response to student writing in front of the class by using the same professor-student writing conference approach. For instance, when a draft of an assignment is due, the professor can ask for a volunteer to read his or her draft to the class. This request can be very intimidating for students, and professors will want to ensure that they treat students with utmost respect when they volunteer to read their drafts.

Once a student volunteers (or is chosen by lot), the professor sits across from the student in front of the class and asks the student to read his or her draft, acknowledging that everyone in the class realizes the writing the student will read is in progress. "We're not expecting you to read a perfect piece of writing to us," the professor might say. Generally, the first reading of the piece allows the professor to glean some ideas about the paper's strengths and some ideas for revising the paper. When I model the professor-student conference in class, I ask the student to read the paper a second time, a bit more slowly. Sometimes, I interrupt the student during the second reading to ask a question. At the end of the reading, I ask the student what he or she thinks about the draft, particularly what the student thinks needs to be done to revise the draft. I also comment about what interested me as a reader, what perplexed me because I need more information, and what suggestions I have for revising the piece.

I have found that these conferences are very helpful to students for three reasons. One, when students read their work aloud, they hear things in the writing that they did not see when they were writing the draft. For instance, they may stumble over a sentence and realize that the sentence does not make sense or they may realize that they omitted a fact that readers need to know to understand a point the students are trying to make. Students "discover that in the act of reading aloud, they themselves hear omissions in their papers, awkward word choices, run-on sentences, sentence fragments, ambiguous sections . . . " (Healy, 1983, p. 267). Two, reading their drafts aloud allows students an opportunity to begin realizing that their writing needs to be revised. Freshmen in particular often believe that a first draft of a writing assignment is pretty close to being finished, requiring but a few jots and tittles to make it acceptable. Public reading with the mentoring of a professor can provide a gentle but insistent message that substantive revision is a necessary part of the writing process. Three, as the professor asks questions of students' writing, students can see what kind of questions readers might ask of writers, and they can begin to ask the same questions in their analysis of their own drafts and in their critique of peers' drafts. The in-class professor-student writing conference, therefore, serves as a model of how student-student writing conferences might work.

Teaching Students How to Be Effective in Group-Group Critiques

The in-class professor-student writing conference is a model not only for student-student writing conferences but also for group-group writing conferences. Collaborative groups, whether comprising two, four, or more students, can read another group's drafts and offer critiques of those drafts to help students revise their writing (Bouton and Tutty, 1975; Harris, 1978; Newman, 1986; Nystrand and Brandt, 1989; Pitts, 1988; Schiff, 1982). (The professor needs to ask each group to provide sufficient copies of a draft for each member of the other group.) To facilitate student critiques, the professor can provide a sheet with questions about the written work (see Figure 4). Students from Group A write answers to the questions based on a critique of Group B's paper, and Group B writes answers to the questions based on a critique of Group A's paper. When both groups have finished the critique, they return the other group's paper to the group along with the critique sheet. Then, after each group has time to review the other group's comments, the groups talk with each other about their papers, clarifying any comments that are not clear and answering questions that the comments may have prompted.

FIGURE 4
A Peer Critique Form

Peer Critique Form for Assignment #3: Dyadic Paper

Name of the persons who wrote the paper _____

Name of the persons who are critiquing the paper _____

1. What is the theme or major point in the dyadic paper?

2. List details in the dyadic paper that support the theme or major point:

   -
   -
   -
   -
   -

3. Are there any places in the dyadic paper where a point does not logically follow a preceding point? If you answer yes, identify those places.

4. Please cite any errors in grammar and mechanics (punctuation, capitalization, and spelling).

5. What other advice would you give to the authors of the dyadic paper to help them revise their paper?

Providing Students with Opportunities for Full-Scale Peer Review

The group-group critique is a prelude to full-scale peer review of penultimate drafts. Peer review can take place between two students who exchange their penultimate drafts with each other or groups of students who exchange drafts. The peer review process is generally more formal than the exchanges between students and groups already discussed. For instance, in peer review, students use a form to answer questions about the draft, similar to the form in Figure 4, but they can also use a grading rubric (discussed later). Peer review is a high-stakes review because students have gone through a series of drafts, have had input from peers and professor, have revised extensively (one hopes), and have had every opportunity to produce a penultimate draft that should be in decent shape. The peer review is therefore a final attempt to provide feedback that will help writers make final changes necessary to produce an excellent document (Sims, 1989).

Conclusion

The range of collaborative writing opportunities that I have discussed is intended to be illustrative. Professors can adapt them to particular classroom situations. In addition, the opportunities I have cited are intended to show professors how they can be mentors and, frankly, collaborators as they work side-by-side with students, preparing them to be successful writers, not only in the classroom but also throughout their careers in various professional fields.

Constructing Collaborative Writing Assignments

WHEN I WAS the coordinator of a writing-across-the-curriculum program, I invited the director of the university writing center to give a presentation to faculty about writing assignments. As the writing center director and I talked about what the presentation might include, he said, "One of the big challenges I face in the writing center is professors' writing assignments." I did not understand what he meant, so he explained, "I ask students who come to the writing center to show me a copy of their professors' writing assignments so that I can check a student's writing with the writing assignment to see where the student needs help. Many times students are not sure what their professors want them to do, and often when students show me a professor's writing assignment, I'm as perplexed as they are about what the professor is asking of them. Then there are the cases where the professor writes an assignment on the board, with cursory instructions, and, again, when I see the student's transcription of the assignment, I'm as perplexed as the student is about what the professor expects. The quality of professors' writing assignments is a big problem when I try to help students improve their writing to meet professors' expectations."

Why did the director of the writing center encounter the recurring problem of vaguely written writing assignments? By and large, faculty across the disciplines have never been given formal training in pedagogy, including the preparation of effective writing assignments, so they create assignments the best they can. They use assignments that seem to work based on models they have picked up along the way or on particular teaching issues they have had to address in their classes. Professors' writing assignments evolve over time as the professors tinker with them, adjusting them based on difficulties students encountered when they attempted to fulfill the assignment and on insights professors gain as they continue to develop as teachers. Writing assignments, therefore, for most faculty are ongoing experiments without the benefit of a sound experimental methodology. In addition, most faculty have no formal training in writing theory. They have not heard about the writing process, and they have never read theoretical arguments concerning the necessity of guiding students through revisions of their writing assignments, of using peer groups to help evaluate writing, and of grading writing effectively. I am not criticizing faculty; I am simply stating a fact of academic life.

I am, however, pointing out the need for this chapter. The director of the writing center had a legitimate problem when he could not help students who came to him—who, perhaps, were sent to him by the professors who created inadequate writing assignments—and handed to him deeply flawed instructions that neither the students nor the director could interpret successfully. Incomplete and fuzzy writing assignments are a disservice to students—and a disservice to those who seek to help students satisfy the requirements of a writing assignment. As Throckmorton (1980, p. 56) says, "A haphazard, slapdash, ill-conceived, or ill-worded assignment invites bad writing, virtually assures capricious grading, and vitiates effective teaching." Professors, therefore, have a responsibility to give students explicit directions about what is expected of them as writers and thus help students achieve high levels of success as writers. That responsibility cannot be fulfilled if professors do not produce effective writing assignments.

Indeed, effective writing assignments are essential when professors consider the complexity of writing tasks. When students write, "they must envision a goal or purpose for writing (often performance) and a rhetorical situation (often that of novice trying to impress expert reader—a difficult situation in which to perform); they must decide on subject and structure (often these elements are determined by the teacher, at least in broad terms); and they must use some process to create the paper (too often combining the techniques of avoidance, of staring blankly at an empty page, and of filling up the blank page with last-minute desperation" (Reiff and Middleton, 1983, p. 266). Reiff and Middleton go on to say that professors may want to create writing assignments "to guide those decisions more carefully" (p. 266).

The need for effective writing assignments is even greater when professors ask students to collaborate in preparing a document because the potential for confusion increases. For a collaborative writing assignment, not only do students encounter the standard problems associated with writing but also they have to work with others to overcome these problems. Collaborative writing assignments have the potential to provide students with tremendous benefits, but those benefits come attached to new challenges—for students and professors.

To provide professors with insights into creating effective collaborative writing assignments to meet some of these challenges, I begin by discussing the writing process so that the entire scope of a writing assignment is before us. Then I explain how to construct *any* writing assignment, realizing that collaborative writing assignments share similar features with single-author writing assignments. After that, I address particular issues related to collaborative writing assignments.

> **Collaborative writing assignments have the potential to provide students with tremendous benefits, but those benefits come attached to new challenges—for students and professors.**

The Writing Process

How a professor conceptualizes the entire writing process has an impact on how he or she understands the role of the writing assignment in that process. If, for instance, a professor conceptualizes the writing process as fairly linear—the professor gives the writing assignment, the students ask questions to clarify the assignment, the students complete the assignment, the professor grades the completed assignments—then the professor will undoubtedly perceive the entire writing process as fairly straightforward, needing little explanation. The professor might assume that students do not need a great deal of detail about the writing assignment because a clear writing assignment will speak for itself, and students should know how to interpret and complete writing assignments. After all, they are college students!

A linear conception of the writing process laden with assumptions about clarity of writing assignments and student facility in fulfilling those assignments is uninformed by composition research. Those who have studied the composing habits of successful student writers (e.g., Beason, 1993; Buechler, 1983; Sommers, 1980), professionals in various fields (e.g., Odell and Goswami, 1985; Spilka, 1993b), and authors who make a living writing (e.g., Waldrep, 1985) have found that writing is not a linear process. Rather, a writer sees some sort of problem, puts preliminary notes on paper to begin addressing the problem, gets troubled by gaps in the ideas he or she is trying to join, asks friends and colleagues what they think about the topic the writer is struggling to articulate, goes to the library and reads what others have said about the topic, reads—sometimes serendipitously—something seemingly unrelated to the topic that nonetheless sheds light on the problem the writer is struggling to solve, writes more, sleeps, eats, showers, writes, comes to another tangle in the writing and asks more questions of friends or experts, reads more in the library, writes, solicits advice from trusted colleagues about how the writing sounds now that something is on paper, revises based on that advice, fills in gaps in the evolving drafts, sleeps, eats, showers, goes to class, buys groceries, writes, and continues this process until time runs out because the assignment is due or, in consultation with trusted readers, determines that the document is worthy of being launched or both. If the launching has in view publication, then the writer goes through the process of peer reviews; revisions based on those reviews, including negotiations about what needs to be revised; more reviews of revised copy; perhaps more revisions; copyediting; proofreading; and, finally, publication.

Certainly, parts of the writing process that I have described can be put in a different order or eliminated. Sometimes, for instance, the writer creates a first or second draft and realizes that he or she has gone the wrong direction, so the draft is dropped in the trash can and the writer begins again. At other times, the writer finds that the writing is coming along well and the need to revise is limited to a few changes in sentences and perhaps the addition of a detail here or there. (Such a situation, though possible, is rare for most writers; see MacNealy, Speck, and Simpson, 1996.) In general, the shorter the document and the more formulaic the format, the less the need for many revisions.

My point, however, is that the writing process is recursive and sloppy, full of loops that take a writer back to previous locations (the library, the thesis statement, the refrigerator), including dead ends. For those who conceptualize the writing process as linear, multiple revisions are seen as arduous and hateful because a linear model predicts that the first draft of a document merely needs tidying up, not successive revisions requiring concentrated efforts struggling with seemingly stubborn language leading to a "final" draft. But LeBlanc (1988) suggests that revision is not one step in the writing process; rather, revision "is located in the whole of the writing process—from point of inscription to final draft" (p. 34). Writing really is revising. Therefore, the linear model, which tries to make writing a lockstep process, just does not work well enough or often enough to create useful and satisfying writing, because the linear model is full of faulty assumptions about how writing gets done. Little wonder that students, untutored in how to manage the writing process and relying upon the linear model, put off the writing task until the night before the paper is due—and often produce dreadful writing. As White (1995, p. 2) notes, "Few students really expect, as they begin college, to produce more than one draft of an essay; many students tend to feel that the first draft is a fully formed text, to be changed as little as possible."

The linear model also predicts that the major problems with writing are surface errors, errors in grammar, spelling, and mechanics. My own experience teaching writing to college students tells me that the major problem with their writing does not stem mainly from their inability to write grammatically correct sentences, to spell correctly, or to know the difference between the contraction *it's* and the possessive pronoun *its*. Sure, some students have trouble writing a grammatically correct sentence, need help with their spelling, and confuse *it's* with *its*. But that is not the major problem for most college students. The major problem is that most students believe that a person who really, really knows how to write writes effortlessly, a fallacy promoted by the linear model. Students, believing that writing is the product of great talent unaided by much effort, have no way to approach the writing task other than to put down ideas as best they can; clean up whatever mistakes in grammar, spelling, and mechanics they see; and turn in their work for the professor's evaluation. Professors reinforce students' writing impotence when they fail to provide students with adequate instruction in the writing process. Writing assignments based on the linear model are examples of such reinforcement;

such writing assignments generally are not very useful in helping students write effectively. So what is to be done?

First, professors need to accept the validity of the process approach to writing. I am not advocating a lockstep approach to writing, as can be seen from the way I outlined the writing process above. No one process will work for every writer. But I am advocating that professors recognize the inherent limitations of the linear model, abandon it, and use a model based on the fruits of composition research. For professors who want to become conversant with the process approach to writing, a large number of works are available (e.g., Elbow, 1981; Flower and Hayes, 1981; Murray, 1991; Rohman, 1965; Sudol, 1982; Zoellner, 1969).

Second, I am recommending that professors incorporate the writing process into the way they approach writing in their classes. For instance, professors should include time to discuss the writing assignment with students, to revise, if necessary, the assignment based on such discussions, to provide opportunities for students to select writing topics and narrow those topics to a manageable size, to review a series of drafts in class, to allow students to critique peers' drafts, to comment on students' "final" drafts and allow students to revise those drafts before they are graded. When professors incorporate the process model of writing into their classrooms, they may have to alter the way they teach their classes. Undoubtedly, they will have to balance issues related to content with issues related to process and determine how process can aid students in learning content. When professors lace their classes with a good dose of process writing, they will find that process and content interact well. Because the first tangible product of a process approach to writing is the writing assignment the professor produces, I now turn to a discussion of how to construct a writing assignment.

The Writing Assignment

The writing assignment is one part of an organic process, so the writing assignment needs to fit that process. In fact, as Connors (1990) reminds us in discussing how to teach technical writing, collaborative writing assignments should promote active learning: "In effective collaborative learning, the teacher defines the task very carefully so that students are given assignments which will stimulate active learning" (p. ET-30). One implication of designing collaborative writing assignments so that they stimulate active learning is that the professor should conceptualize the entire writing process for any particular project before producing a writing assignment. How long will students have to complete the assignment? How many drafts are they required to produce? How will students' writing be evaluated? How does a particular writing assignment fit with the overall objectives of the course? White (1995, pp. 6–7) provides a series of questions that professors can ask when they create writing assignments. Another way to begin answering the questions I posed is to consider two cardinal polestars of writing: purpose and audience.

Purpose

The essential purpose of a writing assignment is to provide students with the opportunity to practice their writing so that they can become more proficient writers. In considering this purpose, the professor will want to question the administrative purpose of grading as the focal point of the assignment. That is, the final grade a professor gives for a particular assignment is not the focal point; rather, the writing assignment should be built around a richer and more complex understanding of evaluation. (For a thorough treatment of grading, see Speck, 2000.)

Although the concept of evaluating writing is imprecise because various terms are used to describe evaluation (i.e., grading, marking, responding to, assessing, commenting on, evaluating; see Speck and Jones, 1998), the professor can bring some clarity to the problem of "grading" by dividing the writing process into two major parts. The first part includes everything that leads up to the final grade. The second part comprises the process of assigning a final grade. The first part is called *formative evaluation,* the second *summative evaluation.*

The purpose of formative evaluation is to provide students with advice about how to improve their written products so that students have the best opportunity to be successful when their work is submitted for summative evaluation. Thus, formative evaluation begins with the writing assignment, because in the writing assignment the professor outlines exact expectations about what students need to do to complete the assignment successfully. Here, then, are pointers about what should be included in a writing assignment.

Purposes. State clearly the *real* purpose of the assignment. Many students believe that the real purpose of an assignment is to get a passing grade. The professor needs to emphasize that the grade is not the real purpose. Rather, the real purpose is to provide students with an opportunity to practice their writing so that they can become better writers, so that they can satisfy the needs of particular audiences. That, however, is a global purpose that fits virtually any writing assignment. What, exactly, will a particular writing assignment require of students so that they master particular skills related to that global purpose? Will the students learn how to conduct research so that they will have a knowledge base for writing an informative report? Will students be asked to marshal evidence to produce a persuasive document? Will students be asked to master a particular form, such as a laboratory report, memo of record, journal article, or letter of recommendation? In other words, what exact skills and what genre are being mandated? The purpose of an assignment might also be to build on existing skills, so the professor should note that a certain level of analysis, for instance, is assumed and that the assignment is intended to extend the students' analytical abilities.

Audience. Most documents are written for multiple audiences, and writing assignments should state explicitly who those audiences might be.

Schedule. When are drafts due? The writing assignment may refer to the syllabus, which includes a detailed schedule, but if such a schedule is not included in the syllabus, it should be included in the writing assignment. In addition, professors can state policies regarding late drafts. The problem of late drafts is particularly thorny when students work on collaborative projects. The schedule also should include opportunities for students to critique peers' drafts.

Requirements. Length of written products, typestyle, use of headings, prohibitions concerning stylistic issues, use of graphics, margins, method of documentation—all these requirements should be stated in the writing assignment. It really is not fair for a professor to ding students for using contractions, for instance, if the professor did not tell students not to use contractions. I am aware of one professor who insists that graduate students staple multipage writing products in the right-hand corner at a 45-degree angle. This is an absurd requirement to my mind, but the professor does tell students the requirement at the beginning of the writing assignment.

Grading. A later chapter is devoted to grading collaborative writing assignments, so a detailed exposition of that topic is included later. At present, however, I simply note that the requirements for grading the final product should be stated explicitly in the writing assignment. As I note later, professors might consider working with students to develop a grading rubric that can be used when the students critique peers' drafts. A grading rubric is a scoring guide that clearly delineates criteria and corresponding rating values that will be used to evaluate students' written products. It allows the grading standards to be used throughout the process so that students have before them the quality standards that will be used during summative evaluation.

When professors prepare a good draft of a writing assignment, it is wise to ask colleagues to review the draft. Asking students to critique the assignment is also an excellent idea. Professors can provide their classes with a clean draft of the assignment, review the assignment with the class, and ask class members to explain the assignment. One technique I use, after going over the assignment in class, is to say, "I missed class today, and I understand that Speck handed out a writing assignment. What does he expect from us?" Then, as students begin to answer my query, I ask dumb questions: "Oh, so can I use pink paper?" My answer to that question, by the way, is, "Anything I didn't specify on the writing assignment is a matter of your choice. Did I specify in the assignment that you had to use a certain color of paper?" In other words, I want the students to know that if I specify something (include four references, only one of which can be an Internet source), then I am laying down an inflexible standard. If I say nothing about the color of paper, students are free to turn in the assignment on whatever color or kind of paper they choose. (Some assignments might merit brown paper sacks, others vellum. I explain to students that they should make choices about paper, for instance, based on the genre, the audience, and the purpose of the document. After all, part of learning to write is learning how to "package" written products.)

Another dumb question might be, "So can I write a one-page paper? That's OK?" Again, unless I specify length requirements in the assignment, students are free to choose the length of their written products. Frankly, the length of students' papers is not an issue once they use the writing process, because they learn how to narrow a topic and write about that topic effectively. Length can become an issue in two ways, however. First, students do not use the writing process effectively and turn in meager, underdeveloped papers. Second, students write so much that the professor is inundated with paper. When used properly, the writing process guards against these two extremes, but no process can guarantee that students who are learning how to write effectively will not succumb either to the call to skimp or to the zealous desire to churn out more and more and more.

Once students have reviewed the writing assignment, possibly raising issues that need clarification, the professor can revise the assignment for clarity or use the draft as the final copy of the assignment. Very likely, the writing assignment will be more than one page, especially if a grading rubric is included. (For those interested in seeing how the process of revising a writing assignment worked in one situation, I recommend Hopson's [1998] recounting of how a writing assignment for a consumer report was revised successfully.)

All that I have said thus far about writing assignments applies to formative evaluation. That is, in the writing assignment, the professor is providing detailed information that aids students in preparing excellent written documents. That detailed information includes a process students can use formally (peer review of drafts, for instance) and informally (personal application of criteria in the writing assignment) to check their progress toward excellence. Not enough has been said, however, about the second pillar of writing—audience—and how audience needs to be treated in the writing assignment.

Audience

Up to this point, I have discussed issues related to the purposes for a writing assignment and ways those purposes can be articulated. Besides purpose, the other pillar of writing is audience. In considering audience, the professor might ask to whom the students are writing. Traditionally, students write to satisfy professorial tastes and criteria, and even when professors introduce other audiences into the assignment (e.g., managers, machine operators, experts), students have the distinct feeling that the professor is really the sole audience for an assignment. Indeed, professors have to be inventive to convince students that they should write for audiences in addition to the professor and to create assignments that realistically allow for the possibility that other audiences will be reading the students' work. Literature is available that addresses ways that professors can help students focus on audiences beyond the classroom. For instance, professors can ask experts to critique students' work (Sawyer, 1975, 1976), have other professors act as critiquers or co-critiquers of students' products (Raymond, 1976; Tritt, 1983), and call upon students in the classroom to critique peers' writing (Speck, 1998a, pp. 45–55). In all these cases, the professor teaching the class helps provide ways for students to receive feedback from audiences other than the professor, reinforcing the concept that students are practicing writing documents for audiences typical of the world beyond the classroom. In addition, Lay (1982) provides questions students can ask from an audience's perspective in revising particular types of documents.

Besides giving students the opportunity to function as audiences for peers' writing, employing students as peer critiquers has the added advantage of allowing students to apply the evaluative criteria to peers' writing during formative evaluation. The writing assignment should include opportunities for students to get responses to their drafts. In small classes, perhaps the professor has time to read preliminary drafts and provide written or oral feedback to each student based on a reading of students' drafts. Professors of small classes may even have the time to conduct student-professor conferences (Speck, 1998a, pp. 31–37). But in medium and large classes, the professor will be hard-pressed to do much more than have students show their drafts to the professor and ask questions about the writing assignment that have surfaced since the students actually began writing to fulfill the assignment. The professor, however, can use students in the class to read and respond to peers' writing. Opportunities in class for students to read and comment on drafts should be included in the writing assignment, because students need to learn how to provide formative feedback to their peers. Why? Students are being prepared to take leadership positions in business and industry, to be, in short, particular types of readers. As leaders, they will be called upon to evaluate others' writing, and professors have some obligation to prepare students for their role as evaluators of writing in business and industry.

Moreover, students can learn about revising by reviewing their peers' writing. The act of reading a piece of writing to provide feedback for revision can be a useful aid in developing a method of critiquing writing. As representatives of diverse audiences, students can bring insights about a peer's writing that can help the peer re-vision the writing and improve it. Thus, students can not only help peers revise their writing but also learn how to apply standards (and, one hopes, internalize those standards) by critiquing others' writing.

> **Students can learn about revising by reviewing their peers' writing.**

Thus far, I have discussed ways to promote formative evaluation, but, clearly, no magic line exists between formative and summative evaluation. All that a professor does to orchestrate students' success and to promote quality writing by providing an excellent writing assignment and following the writing process leads inexorably to summative evaluation—and, one would hope, high rates of success for students who are willing to work diligently under the care of their professors. I have framed the present discussion about the writing assignment in terms of assessment, because the purpose of a writing assignment is to satisfy the quality criteria of particular audiences.

The Collaborative Writing Assignment

All that I have said about the writing assignment applies to collaborative writing assignments, but collaborative writing assignments have particular issues that need to be addressed: What constitutes a group? Who produces what? How is the group graded? I discuss ways professors can form groups in the next chapter and grading in detail in a later chapter, but the question of who produces what is treated here.

If the purpose of a collaborative writing assignment is to help students practice writing to meet the needs of particular audiences, then all the members of a collaborative group need to practice writing. It does not make good pedagogical sense for one student in the group to do all the word processing in lieu of doing any writing. The next chapter suggests ways that professors can monitor a group's activities, but at this juncture, I emphasize the need to make a clear statement in the writing assignment that, although the group will have liberties in terms of assigning the work for a writing project, all members of the group are expected to participate equally in the writing the group does. Thus, a portion of each group member's grade will be determined on the basis of whether the group member did his or her share of the writing. The next chapter explains how the professor can augment information in the writing assignment to explain to students how grading will work, how groups can be formed, and how students can be trained to be effective collaborators.

Forming Groups, Training Students to Be Effective Collaborators, and Managing Collaborative Groups

WHEN I BEGAN using collaborative writing groups years ago, I blithely assumed that once students were in groups they would somehow manage to work together. After all, I saw before me young adults, many of whom had jobs and family responsibilities, so I assumed that they would know the ins and outs of working as a team. Frankly, I did not have well-formed ideas about how to help students be effective collaborators, other than teaching them about the writing process, monitoring that process as students produced drafts, and engaging them in slight conversation about how the group projects were progressing. I treated collaborative writing assignments much as I treated single-author assignments.

I was rudely brought to a halt when groups started to encounter interpersonal conflicts. One person in the group was not carrying his load of the work. Another group member believed that she did not need to attend group meetings. Yet another student always turned in her part of the work late, putting the group behind in its schedule. These and other misdemeanors raised issues about fairness in evaluation. Was it fair for me to give everyone in the group a lower grade because the group's final document suffered through one person's misconduct? But if I tried to sort out exactly who did what for the group and used the resulting information to make evaluation decisions, I saw massive problems in trying to make finely nuanced judgments about students' efforts. (For professors who have struggled with evaluating coauthored publications for tenure and promotion decisions, my quandary about assigning which work to what author may find a sympathetic hearing. In fact, assigning what to whom may be impossible [Anson, Brady, and Larson, 1993;

Morris and Mead, 1995]). I realized that I had painted myself into a corner by not addressing issues related to individual and group responsibilities and linking them to summative evaluation at the outset of the collaborative writing process, so I devised a way to address such issues before the groups began their work. (See the explanation later of the 3 Be's to orient students to collaborative group work.) In addition, I read about collaborative writing and learned even more about how I might help students learn to become effective collaborators. Here, then, are suggestions professors can use to form collaborative writing groups, to provide students with instruction about effective collaboration, and to manage the groups throughout the collaborative writing process.

Forming Groups

What constitutes a group for a collaborative writing assignment? Obviously, the minimum is two, but how many are too many? The size of the group depends, in part, on the type of writing assignment, including the amount of work the professor expects the group to do to complete the assignment. Complex assignments that result in long documents might be candidates for large groups, of say seven. If, however, seven is an outer limit and the professor envisions group projects that require more than seven group members, perhaps the writing assignment is inappropriate. The literature discusses groups of various sizes, from two to twelve (e.g., Forman, 1989; Leverenz, 1994; Meyers, 1986), but, again, the context for a group assignment must be taken into consideration when the number of students in a group is determined. Bosley and Jacobs (1992), for instance, in discussing collaborative writing in philosophy classes, say that the ideal group size is three.

In forming groups, sometimes I have told the class, "I'm stepping out of the class for ten minutes. Here is a sheet of paper. When I come back, please list your group name and the members in the group on the sheet of paper. I recommend that you form into groups of four or five, with equal representation of gender in the group." When I come back, students are in groups. Generally, when I have used this method to form groups, the students have had a chance in class to get to know each other. I also give them the option of changing groups as the project progresses, if another group will take them, but I point out that because groups are going to evaluate each member in the group on the amount and quality of work each member does for the group, groups might be reluctant to admit new members late in the collaborative process. Indeed, late newcomers might be evaluated negatively because they did not have the same opportunities other group members did to work effectively with the group. The approach to forming groups that I have just mentioned certainly appears cavalier, particularly compared with the approaches I will mention momentarily, but students can have a sense of how well they might work with others, and that "sense," although impressionistic, may be correct. The cardinal point to remember in determining the size and composition of groups is that the more people in the group the more complex logistics become; the possibilities for group failure and failure of individuals within the group increase when a group is too large.

In considering group size, one issue that invariably comes up is whether one student can be a group. I have had students come to me after I have initiated a collaborative writing assignment and ask whether they can be a group of one. Generally, a student who objects to participating in a collaborative group explains that his or her experience with collaborative groups has been bad, and he or she does not want to do all the work for the group again. Even if that student is a "group of one," however, he or she *will* do all the work. At least in a group a chance exists of not having to do all the work alone. Each professor needs to determine beforehand whether single-person groups are allowed, but my advice is to assure students who are concerned about being overworked in a group that you have designed the collaborative writing experience so that inequities in workload are addressed throughout the process and when the final grade is calculated. If professors see the wisdom of using collaborative writing groups, then all students should have the opportunity to participate in such groups to gain the educational benefits collaborative learning promises. Later, I discuss the need for a mix of collaborative and single-author assignments, so one solution for students who do not want to be involved in collaborative groups is to show them that they will have opportunities to be evaluated on their own merits but that collaborative learning offers them rewards that they really should not miss.

Another dimension of what constitutes a group is the role of gender in the group's makeup. In terms of gender, the literature provides mixed viewpoints. Tebeaux (1991), for instance, recommends homogeneous groups based on gender. Rehling (1996), however, finds support for gender-balanced groups. Indeed, although Lay (1992) and Sirc (1991) note that men and women have different communication styles, Raign and Sims (1993), on the basis of a study they conducted, provide evidence that men were just as likely as women to use feminine persuasive techniques. The literature does acknowledge problems that can arise because of gender differences, such as stereotyping women as secretaries for the group and men as experts. In addition, gender differences can have a negative impact on women in gender-balanced groups (Flynn and others, 1991). Some have suggested, however, that communication styles based on gender can be integrated so that group members benefit from the strengths of both styles (Atwood, 1992; Burnett and Ewald, 1994; Chiseri-Strater, 1991; Lay, 1989).

The variety of viewpoints about the impact of gender should cause professors to consider the complexity of male-female relationships in classroom writing groups. On the one hand, gender differences can be quite positive. The different viewpoints that females bring to a male perspective and that males bring to a female perspective can be very useful as students analyze the impact of gender on various audiences. Pragmatically, the argument could be made that workplace writing necessitates the interaction of both genders and that students should therefore learn how to work with both men and women. On the other hand, differences in the ways males and females communicate can cause interpersonal conflict, and the literature tends to endorse the belief that women come out on the short end if such conflict is not addressed appropriately.

Clearly, professors need to be sensitive to difficulties resulting from differences in communication styles. Concrete ways exist to express sensitivity to gender issues:

Ensure that the ratio of males to females in a collaborative writing group is balanced as much as possible so that neither gender feels outnumbered.
Discuss the different ways men and women communicate. Markel (1998) notes that "women's communication patterns are more focused on maintaining

the group, and men's on completing the task" (p. 62), so professors might want to use Markel's observation as a starting point for discussing with the class communication styles based on gender.

Establish group roles that contradict gender stereotypes. For instance, if professors want each group to take notes of its meetings, they can ask students to establish a secretary-in-rotation so that every student in the group has the opportunity to be the note taker.

In short, when professors sensitize students to the need to treat men and women with respect, professors send out a strong signal that respect *is* a behavioral requirement for the class.

Another issue related to forming groups is cultural differences. Frankly, the literature on collaborative writing says little about multiculturalism per se, but authors do address concerns about students whose first language is not English. An ongoing concern I have about multiculturalism is that professors may not be aware of and sensitive to the ways students from other cultures approach education (Speck, 1997). For instance, in some cultures, students are expected to memorize the sayings of significant historical figures, and those sayings are repeated without attribution because any literate person in the culture would know to whom a saying should be attributed. In American culture, if someone says "to be or not to be," most literate Americans attribute the saying to Shakespeare. And even if they do not attribute it to Shakespeare, they know that the person saying "to be or not to be" is not the originator of the statement.

This issue of attribution can be a thorny problem when students from other cultures write papers in which failure to make appropriate attribution is labeled as plagiarism. Sometimes the students may not fully comprehend that their cultural style of very loose attribution falls in the category of plagiarism, and when they are accused of cheating, they are dismayed. Whether addressing students from other cultures or students from subcultures within American culture, professors may want to review issues related to plagiarism, and if students from other cultures are in writing groups, professors may want to take time to point out differences in the American understanding of attribution and a looser form of attribution other cultures might consider appropriate.

Although Sigsbee, Speck, and Maylath's (1997) edited volume addresses issues related to oral communication concerning students from other cultures, the points authors in that volume address can be useful for professors who are engaged in teaching writing in their discipline to students from other cultures.

At the heart of what I am saying about integrating students from other cultures into collaborative writing groups is the need for professors to recognize that other cultures do not necessarily espouse the same values that Americans cherish. For instance, both Bosley (1993) and Carson and Nelson (1994) point out that students from other cultures may not believe in the value of group writing as it is used in American classrooms and may not function well in groups because the groups do not operate according to the cultural models of collaboration to which the students are accustomed. This may explain why Allaei and Connor (1990) note that students from other cultures may not feel comfortable making negative comments about a peer's writing. Indeed, students from other cultures might feel that making negative comments about native speakers' writing is presumptuous, given the students' own struggle to acquire facility in English.

The problems I have cited are not insuperable, however. To help solve these problems, Bosley (1993), for instance, recommends that professors prepare students from other cultures for collaboration by providing all group members with readings on cultural differences and talking about those differences with the class. Perhaps professors could invite a colleague with expertise in cultural differences to address the class, making students aware of various cultural perspectives on any particular issue. Another suggestion is for the professor to assign someone in the group to mentor the student from another culture, someone who willingly wants to be a helper. This step could enhance group cohesion as well as provide the student from another culture with a ready contact for answering cultural questions, for instance, about the meaning of idioms. Wachholz (1996) recommends that professors bring their own writing to class for review so that students from other cultures see that it is acceptable to critique the written work of authority figures. In fact, native students also could benefit from such a critique. The take-home point about integrating students from other cultures into collaborative writing groups is that the literature provides ways for professors to help such students learn how to be effective group members in American culture, but the professor needs to be sensitive to cultural issues and want to help students from other cultures. In fact, professors need to set the tone of cultural sensitivity so students recognize that acts of cultural sensitivity *are* behavioral requirements.

Yet another issue related to forming groups is writing ability (Rothstein-Vandergriff and Gilson, 1988). The problem of ensuring that groups have a mixture of writing abilities so that the less-experienced writers are not gathered in one group is difficult. First, a professor has to have some reasonable way to determine students' writing ability, which can be a real problem if collaborative groups are initiated early in the class before a professor has adequate time to ascertain students' writing abilities. Certainly, a writing sample solicited by a prompt, for instance, at the beginning of the class could be useful in determining students' writing abilities, but such a sample would have to pass standards of validity and reliability to give professors accurate information about grouping students according to various writing abilities. In addition, the scoring of such writing tests would have to be valid and reliable; for a professor to make impressionistic judgments about students' writing based on students' writing samples is generally not considered valid and reliable. Yet such impressionistic judgments are probably the major method professors use to determine students' writing ability, given the time constraints of a semester or quarter. Further, the type of writing sample is important. A narrative writing sample will not necessarily give professors good information about students' ability to write persuasive or analytic documents, so the mode of the writing sample has implications for determining (or not determining) students' writing ability in other modes. In short, *good* writing is good, given particular requirements. There really is no such thing as universally *good* writing. A person who writes superb research reports might produce a poor personal essay. Professors who seek to determine students' writing ability in any methodologically sound way will find that they spend quite a bit of time and effort to gauge students' writing ability. If professors have access to a service on campus that can provide evidence of students' writing ability, professors' time and effort can be minimized.

Tests that determine whether students know how to identify subjects and verbs are not *writing* tests. They are tests of identification. As such, they do not tell professors much about a student's writing ability.

Second, professors will want to ensure that weaker writers, if they can be identified before the collaborative writing assignment, are required to write as part of their group duties. Better writers in the group might easily usurp the writing role, believing that, for the good of the group and its grade, they should do the bulk of the writing. After all, it is generally easier to write, if you are a good writer, than to help someone else be a better writer, and students may not see that they do have some responsibility to help students in their group become better writers. As Cooper, Robinson, and McKinney (1994) note, "Structures must be built into the learning environment to ensure that all members of a cooperative learning team feel a sense of responsibility for their teammates" (p. 75). Cooper, Robinson, and McKinney use passive voice ("structures must be built"), but clearly, the professor builds those structures, and the next section of this chapter points out how professors can do so.

Certainly, professors can organize collaborative writing groups according to other criteria, such as students' interest in a particular topic, personality types as identified by the Myers-Briggs Type Indicator (Collins, 1989; Jensen and DiTiberio, 1984; Spiegelhalder, 1983), compatibility of students' schedules for out-of-class meetings (Summers and Redmen, 1989), age (Scheffler, 1992), or academic major or subdiscipline (such as accounting). Depending on the amount of time professors have determined that they can spend in testing students, either for writing ability or for personality type, professors can help promote effective group collaboration by forming groups using good data. Because groups are dynamic, however, simply forming groups based on reasonable criteria and good data is no guarantee that the groups will function effectively throughout the collaborative process. Therefore, professors need to train students to be effective collaborators. For instance, professors need to ensure that they communicate behavioral expectations to students concerning interpersonal relationships. Professors can send a strong message that gender, cultural diversity, and various writing abilities are part and parcel of corporate life for collaborative writing groups and as such should be dealt with respectfully. The task of communicating behavioral expectations is our next order of business.

Training Students to Be Effective Collaborators

As I pointed out at the beginning of this chapter, when a professor assumes that students will automatically work well together and provides little or no training in group success, groups can fall apart, so professors need to give students guidance about how to work effectively in classroom collaborative writing groups. Does this mean that the professor has to become versed in small-group dynamics? Although the literature on small-group dynamics can yield insights about group behavior, professors can be successful in training and managing collaborative groups with a modest amount of insight into the problems groups might encounter and solutions students can use to address those problems. Thus, this section is based on a problem-solution approach to training students to work effectively as collaborators.

Before addressing specific problems and solutions, however, I emphasize the need for professors to train students at the outset of the collaborative writing experience. I recommend that the training be linked with both formative and summative evaluation, because students can then see the connection between behavior and evaluation. As I affirm in the chapter on grading, students should be provided with evaluative criteria in the early stages of a writing assignment so that they can compare their written products throughout the writing process with the evaluative criteria. And the criteria for a collaborative writing assignment include each student's ability to interact well with the other members of the group—particularly when a professor decides that the written product the group produces will be assigned one grade and that each member of the group will receive that grade. Certainly, other grading schemes are possible, but a major issue related to grading focuses on the ability of the group to work effectively as a group to produce a high-quality document. When a group fails to work together effectively, generally the quality of the document the group produces suffers from group dysfunction. The quality of group interaction and the quality of the document the group produces are inextricably bound together. Thus, the evaluation of the document becomes in large part an evaluation of the group's effectiveness. In some cases, a desperate and talented student may rescue a group from producing a poor document by doing the lion's share of the work, but the quality of such a document masks the group's dysfunction, and rewarding all members of the group equally would be inappropriate. Therefore, issues of fairness in evaluating collaborative writing projects are related to group interaction, and professors do students a service when they warn students about possible problems in group interaction that can derail the goal of producing a high-quality document and when they provide students with techniques for addressing those problems.

> **The quality of group interaction and the quality of the document the group produces are inextricably bound together.**

I see three major problems that can occur in collaborative writing groups. The first problem is leadership. Students may wonder who's in charge. The second problem is conflict resolution. Students may ask how they can get along with people they do not like and who disagree with them. The third problem is work ethic. Students may ask what to do if a group member is not pulling his or her load, either by not attending group meetings or by turning in work late.

Leadership

The chief leader in the classroom is the professor. Sometimes the literature on collaborative learning and collaborative writing may give the impression that the classroom would work just fine if professors stepped outside and let the students get their work done. In fact, those who enthusiastically endorse the student-centered classroom can give the misimpression that professors are peripheral to the classroom. Nothing could be farther from the truth. Bailey and Dyck (1990) confirm the necessity of the teacher's authoritative role in the collaborative classroom when they break down the teacher's responsibilities into four stages: "(1) preliminary decisions, (2) setting the lesson, (3) monitoring and intervening, and (4) evaluating and processing" (p. 40). They also include Johnson and Johnson's substages, such as deciding on group size, assigning students to groups, explaining criteria for success, and evaluating student learning. In a review of studies about effective teaching, Rushton,

Murray, and Paunonen (1983) found that "the picture of the successful college teacher is of a person who is a dynamic, sociable, warm, emotionally stable, responsible leader" (p. 97). Clearly, the professor plays a major authority role in the classroom, and when professors fail to use their authority properly, students can suffer. I begin this discussion of leadership in collaborative writing groups, then, by affirming the necessity of professorial leadership and authority.

Professors have three types of authority—official authority, subject-matter expertise, and teaching authority (Speck, 1998b)—and the professor needs to use all three types of authority effectively for collaborative writing groups to be successful. Professors have official authority because they are agents of the institutions that pay them. Professors are required, for instance, to turn in grades for students in partial fulfillment of their official authority. Professors are expected to have subject-matter expertise, and academic credentials are evidence of that expertise. In addition, professors are assumed to have teaching authority, the ability to teach effectively. Soder (1996), however, notes that it is an untested assumption that "majoring in one of the academic fields prepares one to teach and model and exemplify civic education" (p. 256). This assumption has been severely challenged in a variety of ways in the last decade, and higher education has attempted to respond to criticism of teaching authority by instituting programs whereby graduate students receive instruction in pedagogy as preparation for careers as professors, by creating centers for faculty development with heavy stress on teaching effectiveness, by encouraging faculty to make self-evaluations of their teaching as part of their ongoing development as pedagogues, and by instituting posttenure review.

Another attempt to address the problem of teaching authority comes from advocates of collaborative and active learning. In essence, those who support collaborative learning, active learning, and collaborative writing are saying that the professor's teaching authority is to be used to enable students to participate in democratic decision making, not only in the classroom but also beyond the classroom. This goal requires a hierarchy of authority, however, for at least two reasons. First, hierarchy of some sort is inherent in the human condition. Some people are born with particular abilities that others do not possess or possess but in lesser amounts. Some people work harder than others and thus gain positions of power and influence that even people with great abilities do not have. To suggest, therefore, that everyone is equal in every possible way is quite unrealistic. Hierarchies of various sorts are part and parcel of human existence. The central issue is not whether hierarchies exist—they do and should—but how they can be used to promote democratic principles. As Campbell (1996) says so well, "The classroom is never more democratic than when students and instructor stand on equal footing, though on different rungs of the ladder of mastery, before the common rules of the craft" (p. 218). In other words, the "teacher is not another student; the role carries special responsibilities. It does not entail power over the students; however, it does carry authority, an authority based not on subordination but on cooperation" (Belenky, Clinchy, Goldberger, and Tarule, 1986, p. 227).

Second, in terms of education, "we cannot accept the notion that everyone has an innate sense of democracy, political constitution, and rights and responsibilities, and that everyone is thus free to engage in talk of these matters without expecting to do any heavy lifting" (Soder, 1996, p. 262). Students do not by nature have a vast storehouse of knowledge or necessarily have the drive to acquire knowledge that they lack. Soder explains what he means by "heavy lifting": "Mystery writer Harry Kemelman tells about his protagonist, Rabbi Small, dealing with college students during the first class session. The students are shocked to find that there will be required reading, and that there will be lectures. Why not have a discussion course, says one student. The rabbi considers, shakes his head, and says, 'You mean that by combining your ignorance, you'll be able to achieve knowledge?' No, he says, 'let's proceed in the traditional way. When you have some knowledge, then perhaps we can discuss its interpretation'" (pp. 262–263).

In other words, someone in the classroom needs to provide ideas as a basis for students to examine those ideas and examine their own ideas about those ideas. This does not mean that the professor's job, in a collaborative learning classroom, is to insist that students accept certain ideas. Rather, the professor's job is to create an environment in which ideas can be evaluated, challenged, and modified so that students, of their own choosing, can reject or embrace particular ideas. "The knowledge business should not be just the territory of competing scholars or experts," MacGregor (1990) affirms. Rather, "the shaping and testing of ideas is something in which anyone can participate" (p. 23). To suggest that students simply "create" knowledge out of thin air or solely from their experiences, however, is to suggest that students need no mentoring, no purposeful direction in their analysis of ideas. Such a position contradicts the whole notion of collaboration as learning based on knowledge that already exists. And to provide students with a background, with ideas, with the collaborative knowledge that many others have synthesized, requires an expert mentor—the professor—who has authority and uses it to promote active learning. At the same time, the professor's authority should not be sharply distinctive from students' authority; as Campbell said, professor and students stand on the same ladder. The professor's authority, therefore, should promote blurred distinctions between professorial authority and student authority so that, as Whipple (1987) affirms, "the power line is easily crossed" (p. 4). At the same time, Whipple avers that classroom collaboration does preserve distinctions: "A good family does not dissolve the individuality of its members, but provides a base of support upon which the individualities of its members can rest. Successful collaboration can do the same" (p. 5). The professor therefore uses his or her authority effectively when he or she is not the sole authority in the classroom.

Although the three types of professorial authority—official authority, subject-matter expertise, and teaching authority—can be analyzed separately, they are interrelated, and collaborative writing projects, especially group projects that require students to produce a major document, raise issues about the professor's authority. Some students worry that the professor may give away his or her official authority to groups, especially when group members are asked to evaluate each other. Other students worry that the professor may be abdicating teaching authority by putting more stress on group work and encouraging students to help each other inside and outside class. In addition, students may be concerned that professors will not allow groups to have any real authority, assuming that professors have few ways to effectively delegate authority in the classroom. Thus, "it is not unusual to encounter student resistance to group work. Embedded in student expectations about classroom culture, and in the inertia of their own ingrained habits, such resistance is real and should be taken seriously" (MacGregor, 1990, p. 25). So the question of authority needs to be addressed early in collaborative writing projects.

I recommend that professors state explicitly at the outset of a collaborative writing project the relationship between their authority and the authority they invest in individual students and groups. For instance, the professor can say to students, "I want you to be clear about the relationship between your responsibilities as individuals and as groups, and my responsibility as the teacher of this course. As you can see from the writing assignment, I am giving groups latitude in selecting topics, determining workload, and scheduling meetings. At the same time, I am asking group members to be responsible in treating other group members respectfully, in submitting their work on time, in faithfully attending group meetings, and in fully participating in the life of the group. As I pointed out in the writing assignment, members of the group will have the responsibility to evaluate each other's efforts in relation to the group effort, and I will take into account those evaluations when I assign a grade for the documents you produce. But I want you to know that I take ultimate responsibility for grading the final documents. I have put in place safeguards so that the groups will be able to work effectively—if group members fulfill their responsibility—and I fully expect that the groups, barring any unforeseen disaster, will work smoothly and produce excellent documents."

Professors need to tailor their explanation of authority to the way they structure groups and delegate authority, but students, I have found, want to know that they are not being thrown into a group situation that might either harm their grade point average or cause them to work harder than everyone else in the group to get a decent grade. Thus, I affirm that authority in the classroom flows from the professor and that the professor can delegate (or share) that authority with students, but that the ultimate responsibility for the way the professor uses his or her authority, including delegating authority to students, rests with the professor.

In considering how to delegate authority, one of the questions professors might want to consider is whether to assign a formal leadership role to a student or students in a collaborative writing group. Professors can consult George's (1984) research in answering this question. George categorized collaborative writing groups as one of three types: Task-Oriented, Leaderless, or

Dysfunctional. Of the Task-Oriented group, George says, "The Task-Oriented group is both self-starting and self-perpetuating. Given nearly any task, this group will immediately begin to look for a way to work together. More often than not, these groups are not dominated by a single strong student. In fact, they may not even contain the best writers in the class. Their real strength lies in their willingness to talk and to listen to each other. Because of this openness, they will draw reluctant members into the discussion so that eventually the group really has no reluctant members" (p. 321).

The second type of group, the Leaderless group, according to George, does not exchange ideas, and during in-class group meetings, members of the group often look as though they are reading alone. The Leaderless group, "though literally without a leader, can easily be dominated by one group member who consistently passes judgment quickly and forcefully and cuts other comments off immediately. This dominant member does not allow for the kind of strong exchange of views characteristic of successful group inquiry" (p. 321).

The Dysfunctional group does not function at all as a group. "They are not self-starting. They have difficulty beginning work on even the simplest of tasks. They cannot keep a discussion moving" (p. 321).

George's description of groups based on her research does not help professors assign group leaders; rather, what George's description does is alert professors to the fact that leadership in a group may arise spontaneously. This spontaneous manifestation of leadership militates against scientific notions that if professors have enough data, they can form effective groups. Indeed, time constraints and paucity of data may very well hinder professors from forming groups based on precise methodologies governed by scientific principles. The professor's dilemma, then, is what to do in the face of time constraints and inadequate data when forming groups and selecting leaders for those groups. I have found no easy answer to this dilemma, but here are some possible ways to address the problem of group leadership:

Do not appoint a leader. Form groups based on whatever data are readily available (writing samples, previous experience with students who have taken your other classes, grade point averages, comments from colleagues about students' abilities, and so on), hope that leadership arises naturally, and plan to monitor groups extensively during the collaborative writing process to provide effective leadership.

Appoint formal group leaders. Summers and Redmen (1989) recommend that professors appoint students with leadership experience to positions of leadership in a collaborative writing group. One way to gather data about students' leadership abilities is to ask students to provide personal data about jobs they have had, leadership positions in social organizations, parental responsibilities, desire for leadership, and so forth. Then professors can consult this data to appoint formal leaders.

Appoint students to informal roles of leadership. One way to approach this problem of group leadership is not to think about it in terms of a leader, but to think about the tasks a group needs to accomplish and make sure that someone has responsibility to ensure the group gets those tasks accomplished. A professor, therefore, could select a person to be the scheduler, to ensure that the group keeps on schedule. The scheduler could make periodic reports to the professor so that the professor can determine whether a particular group needs help in getting its work done on time.

Ask the group to select a leader. The success of a group in selecting a leader may depend on how familiar group members are with each other. In freshman courses, students may not know anyone in the class initially and may have passing familiarity with some of their peers toward the end of the class. In upper-division courses in the major, students may have taken courses with other students and know several peers well enough to determine whether a particular group member would be a good leader. Of course, the size of the school or university may have an impact on how familiar students are with their peers. In a large research university, incoming freshmen, for instance, may have few classes with the same students, and even if a student has a peer in more than one course, the courses may be large lecture sections. So students under those conditions may not have sufficient knowledge to make an informed decision about selecting a group leader.

Ask students to volunteer for a leadership role. Again, professors can ask students to provide information about previous leadership roles and a statement about why they would want to lead a group. Students might, however, volunteer for a leadership role, not with the intention of leading, but with the intention of taking over the group. For instance, a student who wants to ensure that the project is done "right" might volunteer to lead the group and then do most of the work. Although some group members might think such a situation optimal, it militates against the philosophy of collaborative learning/writing. In addition, students may see themselves as leaders when in fact they are not. Thus, evidence of leadership ability in other contexts can be useful in selecting volunteers.

Issues related to group leadership are either easily solved or hard to resolve, from my experience with collaborative writing projects. When leadership is not a problem, a group, under the professor's guidance, generally works well together. Leadership of some sort arises, whether one person becomes a spokesperson for the group or two people work together to provide leadership. Sometimes no one person is the leader, but the group members are mature enough that they individually do their work and produce a good document. Such groups are the Task-Oriented groups George identified.

At other times, groups suffer from student leadership. The person the group selected to be a leader is not working out. By the time I find out that the leadership is weak, the project may be well under way, and I may have to intervene by becoming the quasi–group leader, at least in terms of pulling students together and giving them concrete suggestions for completing the project: "Well, if Theobald is having trouble meeting with the group for the regular Tuesday evening meetings," I might say, "can you all agree on another meeting time? Let's take a look at your schedules." In a follow-up conversation, I will ask how the new meeting time is working out. In some cases, students just have not thought about how to solve problems, and the problems can therefore become bigger than they actually are. In other cases, the problems are big, and even good student leaders may need professorial intervention. Zelda has dropped out of school. She was supposed to provide the critical analysis of the data, and she has not done any analysis. Such a crisis is manageable, if professors and students are willing to be flexible, shift the workload, maybe reconceptualize the project, and perhaps allow the project to be turned in after the due date.

My point is that groups are dynamic, and all the efforts professors invest in groups may not anticipate leadership and personnel issues that can have a marked influence on the group's performance. As George (1984) notes, collaborative group work "forces teachers to constantly listen, constantly watch, constantly suggest. . . . They must . . . come prepared to work through problems that naturally arise within the context of such a class" (p. 325). This does not mean, of course, that professors should not do their utmost at the outset of a project to plan for collaborative writing groups to be successful. Rather, they should recognize that they have the ultimate authority in the classroom. Although they need to delegate authority by allowing students to demonstrate their abilities as evaluators, subject-matter experts, and teachers, the professor has a unique responsibility to help collaborative writing groups be successful, and that responsibility may include rescuing a group that is floundering.

Conflict Resolution

Another responsibility professors have is to alert groups to potential conflicts that may arise in the group, and Jehn (1997) provides a useful model for the types of intragroup conflict that can occur: task, relationship, and process. Task conflict refers to disagreements about what needs to be done. Relationship conflict refers to problems group member have "with others' personalities and dispositions" that do "not focus on task issues" (p. 540). For example, one group member, for whatever reason, simply dislikes another group member. Process conflict refers to "conflict about how task accomplishment should proceed in the work unit, who's responsible for what, and how things should be delegated" (p. 540). In other words, groups can experience conflict about what needs to be done, who does what, and who grates on whom.

In addition, Jehn discusses group norms—"standards that guide group members' behavior" (p. 544). Such norms, if they do not endorse high levels of conflict, can promote task conflict or frank discussion about what needs to be done, enhancing group effectiveness. Burnett (1994) agrees and found that "co-authors who considered more alternatives and voiced more disagreements about content and other rhetorical elements . . . produced higher quality documents than co-authors who considered few or no alternatives and voiced little or no explicit disagreements" (p. 240). (See also Burnett, 1991, 1993.) Others endorse the need for positive task conflict (Ewald and MacCallum, 1990; Johnson and Johnson, 1979; Karis, 1989; Schreiber, 1996). In addition, group norms that discourage both relationship and process conflicts also enhance group effectiveness, partly because the negative emotions that are part of relationship and process conflicts are not allowed. Thus, "the optimal profile for high-performing groups includes important, moderate task conflicts, no relationship conflicts, and little or no procedural conflict, with norms that task conflict is acceptable and resolvable and with little negative emotionality" (Jehn, 1997, p. 552).

Jehn's model provides professors with a theoretical basis for approaching conflict resolution and reinforces the need for professors to establish group norms for the class, which the professor can do quite easily. Concerning what needs to be done, the professor clearly articulates in the writing assignment the nature of the writing project (the task), even discussing subtasks (e.g., brainstorming, researching, drafting, reviewing, editing, and proofreading). Concerning who does what (the process), the professor can determine whether groups should have official leadership. If they do, the professor can work with the leaders to see that group subtasks are assigned equitably. (Again, Figure 3 is a concrete way to have students record in proposal format who does what.) Concerning who grates on whom (the relationship), the professor can do two things.

First, the professor can announce that interpersonal conflict based on negative attitudes and feelings about a group member have no place in the group. For instance, professors can say, "If you find that you don't like someone in the group, deal with it outside the group either by keeping it to yourself or approaching the person on your own time and expressing your attitude in a nonthreatening way. You may, for example, see a group member as insufferably arrogant, and you may be correct in your analysis, but your attitude and feelings about that person's arrogance should not become a cause of conflict in the group. If, however, the person's arrogance is the cause of conflict because the person's expression of arrogance is in conflict with group norms about acceptable behavior, then the group should address the problem as it relates to the task at hand, *not* as arrogance relates to the group's disgust of such a personality trait."

Second, the professor can announce that politeness and reasoned discourse are norms when groups discuss how to complete the task at hand. The professor can tell the class, "Each group member has both the right and responsibility to express his or her viewpoints about how to best promote the work of the group. Each group member has the responsibility to listen carefully when other group members exercise their right and responsibility to express their viewpoints about how to best promote the work of the group. At times, group members may disagree about the best way to promote the group's work. That's fine, but all such disagreements must be presented using reasonable language—not name calling, ridicule, sexist remarks, or ethnic slurs. And *all* viewpoints should be treated with respect. If anyone in the group violates the two group norms for addressing group conflict, the rest of the group should stop the conversation and firmly but politely repeat the two norms: use reasonable language and treat *all* viewpoints with respect. If the group needs someone to be an arbitrator about whether these group norms have been violated, just call on me to be an umpire."

I stress the need for professors to deal openly with politeness because a common perception of emotions in American culture is that people have the right to express themselves, and if a person is genuinely expressing emotions that constitute rude behavior, such expressions are to be accepted. Sincerity becomes the touchstone for determining genuine emotions, even if those emotions are negative. That perception of emotions can be dangerous in groups, and I recommend that professors head off the negative effects groups could experience from individual members acting on such a perception. Thus, the professor's frank announcement of group norms concerning relationship and process conflicts can be very effective in setting a positive tone for group behavior, but the professor also needs to provide students with techniques for dealing with intragroup conflict. These techniques can be grouped under two headings: administration of group meetings and interaction among group members.

Administration of Group Meetings.

Establish group roles. Previously, I discussed roles group members might assume, such as secretary-in-rotation and group leader. Group members can serve in a number of other roles, however. For instance, Flower and Ackerman (1994) discuss the roles of group leader, planning coordinator, recorder, and devil's advocate (p. 247). Hulbert (1994) lists eleven group roles, including gatekeeper, encourager, information giver, and summarizer. According to Hulbert, each group member can fulfill each role. The value of group roles for everyone in the group is that everyone has a job to do. Ensuring that each member does his or her job is another matter, but group roles can foster inclusion, commitment, and efficiency, thus helping to minimize negative conflict.

Require frequent group meetings. Nelson and Smith (1990) recommend frequent group meetings as a way to minimize conflict. Their suggestion makes sense if group norms regarding positive ways to deal with conflict are in place and if group members subscribe to those norms. Otherwise, frequent group meetings could be painful and harmful to the group. Frequent group meetings, however, also can allow group members adequate time to plan, to work on, and to complete their project. How many meetings constitute "frequent" depends on the nature of the project and the time allotted for the project.

Singing in tune is one way to promote group harmony and minimize the dissonance of negative conflict.

Ask students to provide you with an agenda for group meetings, meeting minutes, and progress reports (Ewald and MacCallum, 1990). Whether professors want to ask groups for agendas, meeting minutes, and progress reports depends, in part, on how much information the professors want from each group. In addition to keeping professors informed about potential intra-group conflicts, however, all three documents can help group members to practice organizational and reporting skills that are typical of the skills groups use in business, industry, and the academy. In addition, such documents provide "objective" data, helping group members ensure that they are all singing from the same musical score. Singing in tune is one way to promote group harmony and minimize the dissonance of negative conflict.

Interaction Among Group Members

Introduce students to collaborative planning. Conflicts can arise easily at the beginning of a project when students are trying to establish direction for the project. In addition to the uncertainty of how the group is going to function, students may also have anxiety about how the work is going to get done. Collaborative planning—constructing effective plans to achieve their goal—is one way to help reduce students' anxiety that might lead to conflict. Collaborative planning requires part of the group to be writers or planners and part of the group to be supporters. (Or all groups could function as planners. Then groups could be paired and one group could function as supporters for the other group and vice versa.) Planners create an initial plan for the group's project, and supporters provide oral feedback for the plan. One reason that collaborative planning is so useful is that oral feedback can be extremely helpful in giving peers guidance (Johnson and Johnson, 1986; Plowman, 1993; Radcliffe, 1972). Collaborative planning also can be very useful in helping groups prepare to accomplish the task before them and thus minimize conflict that can arise because of poor planning. As Burnett (1993) notes, "Writers who use collaborative planning can provide each other with the support necessary to plan and draft more skillfully than they could have done independently" (p. 129). Professors interested in learning more about collaborative planning will find a rich literature at their disposal (Brown-Guillory, 1987; Brozick, 1992; Flower and Ackerman, 1994, pp. 142–147; Flower and Higgins, 1991; Flower, Wallace, Norris, and Burnett, 1994; Higgins, Flower, and Petraglia, 1990; Lewis, 1993; Plowman, 1993).

Use student journals. Goldstein and Malone (1984, 1985) suggest that professors ask students to keep personal journals in which students record their group interaction experiences. Professors read the journals periodically and offer solutions, when necessary, to group conflicts. (See also Roebuck, 1988; Lay, 1989, 1992.)

Provide students with decision-making tools. When group members use planning and time management tools, they can lessen conflict that is the result of poor planning. Flower and Ackerman (1994) recommend a variety of decision-making tools for this very purpose, including milestones, Gantt charts, the Standard Agenda, the Delphi method, Task Tables, and Critical Path Charts (pp. 250–265).

Explain negotiation techniques. Conflict can arise because of misunderstandings, and the various techniques I have cited share the purpose of making explicit the issues groups need to address. Thus, the techniques are ways to negotiate the group's understanding of a project. Professors may want to focus, however, on two negotiating techniques that are foundational to all the other techniques: *active listening* and *effective questioning*. Active listening simply means that group members concentrate on what a group member is saying and then repeat what the group member said: "So I hear you saying that we should all write individual drafts of the paper and then make those separate drafts into one cohesive draft. Is that correct?" Asking for confirmation of the interpretation of what the group member said is critical, because asking for confirmation gives the group member an opportunity to acknowledge that the interpretation is correct or to explain in what ways the interpretation does not square with the group member's ideas. Effective questioning follows from active listening if group members find that they have more questions about a proposal or idea or want to explore its pros and cons. For instance, if one group member advances the idea that all group members should create separate drafts of the project so that the group can meld those drafts into one text, other group members could ask questions about the proposal. One type of question is a what-if question: "What if just two group members prepare a draft and the rest of the group critiques that draft to create one draft for the entire group?" What-if questions allow the group to explore other alternatives related to the proposal at hand. Another type of question is the rhetorical question: "Wouldn't we waste quite a bit of time if we each create a draft?" The group member who made the proposal that each group member create a draft might not consider such a question rhetorical and give various reasons why individual drafts of the project would be beneficial to the group. In other words, the group member who makes the proposal might perceive what was intended to be a rhetorical question as a question of clarification, realizing that he or she had not given sufficient reasons why individual drafts are good for the group. In all the negotiations in which the group engages, professors will want to reinforce the need for civility—for the group to focus on tasks, not personalities—when they actively listen and ask various questions. I will say more about negotiation when I address group interaction during the revision stage of the writing process.

In briefly discussing techniques that groups can use to address potential conflicts productively, my intention is to provide a sample toolkit professors can consult when they seek to help students prepare to be effective collaborators. More can be said about conflict management, and much has been written about that topic. For professors interested in reading more about conflict management, I recommend the references Jehn (1997) cites as a place to begin a thorough study of literature on conflict management. The following section addresses how to help students think about their need to establish a productive work ethic—both as individual group members and as a group.

Work Ethic

I have found, and the literature on collaborative writing confirms (e.g., Trzyna and Batschelet, 1990), that one of the major conflicts groups encounter has to do with work ethic. A pressing question for most students is whether they will have to do more than their share of the work to produce a document. Therefore, professors should provide procedural and behavioral guidelines that address this concern. I have incorporated both types of guidelines in a handout I devised called "The 3 Be's of Collaborative Writing" (Figure 5). I present the 3 Be's to the entire class after they have formed groups. I offer the 3 Be's here as one method professors can use to stress the necessity of individual group members and the group itself adopting a work ethic that honors meeting deadlines and interacting with respect toward other group members. The 3 Be's, therefore, not only stress the necessity of a strong work ethic but also reinforce the need for conflict management.

Be Responsible (as an Individual). If individuals do not take responsibility for their part of the group effort, the group will suffer and the quality of the group's written product will probably suffer. Individual responsibility, although not beginning with meeting deadlines, is often proved by meeting deadlines, so I note at the outset the importance of meeting deadlines. I also point out to students that the class syllabus, which includes all the deadlines for every project in the course, should not leave them in doubt about when projects are due.

FIGURE 5
Procedural and Behavioral Guidelines for Collaborative Writing Groups

The 3 Be's of Collaborative Writing

Be Responsible (as an Individual)
- Meet deadlines
- Schedule sufficient time to make quality a priority
- Plan, plan, plan—including planning for problems

Be Organized (as a Group)
- Prepare a schedule and monitor it as the project progresses
- Complete assignments on time
- Counsel group members who are late to meetings and who do not understand the meaning of *dead*line

Be Honest
- Tell group members what you can and cannot do
- Express your reservations about the way the group is approaching the project
- Counsel weak group members

The next point under Be Responsible (as an Individual) is a comment about the relationship between time and quality. Again, the class syllabus lists dates when the first draft, second draft, third draft for peer critique, and fourth draft of the project are due. Professors whose style of teaching is not amenable to such detail in the syllabus may want to ensure that students schedule due dates for drafts. As a rule, I have found that students are very busy and that they tend to respond to the pressures of the moment. One implication of their crisis management styles is that writing gets done at the last minute. Yet last-minute writing is merely first-draft writing, not presentation copy. Therefore, students need to be shown how to schedule time to make quality a priority in their writing. Figure 3 is an example of one way to get students to schedule their writing activities so that they have a fighting chance to achieve particular standards of quality. The second point under Be Responsible (as an Individual) reinforces the need for scheduling time—both personal and group time devoted to the project—to ensure that written products are acceptable.

The third point—plan, plan, plan—including planning for problems—is designed to forewarn students about potential disruptions. Gretchen may break a leg and not be able to do all the work she intended to do. Hansen may get the flu and be bedridden for a week, during the time when he was supposed to write the third section of the report. I'm not asking students to predict such events, unless, of course, a student knows that he or she is scheduled for dental surgery the week when the final draft is scheduled for group scrutiny. I am asking them to add enough flexibility in their planning so that they have some wiggle room. One way to add that wiggle room is to plan backwards.

Students know when the project is due. That date is on the syllabus. So they know that the day before the project is due they need to have the presentation copy virtually completed. The day before that they should have made the last-minute changes and meticulously read the resulting copy. The day before that they should have. . . . When students have built a schedule backwards to Day 1, they should tighten the schedule by 10 percent. That is, they should move the schedule back by 10 percent of the time they have allotted for the project so that the due date is 10 percent earlier than the scheduled due date. This tightening will allow for unforeseen events—Gretchen's broken leg and Hansen's flu—that have the potential to wreck havoc with the project. Planning for problems is not merely a group issue. Individual students need to plan for unforeseen problems so they can complete their work for the group—on time.

Be Organized (as a Group). Under the first Be, I mixed group and individual responsibility because I find them hard to separate, unless one person does extraordinary work or one person fails miserably and puts the group project in jeopardy. One of my goals in presenting the 3 Be's to students is to get them to think about the intertwining of individual and group effort. Thus, under Be Organized (as a Group), I reinforce this intertwining nature of individual and corporate responsibility. The first point under Be Organized (as a Group) reinforces the notion of scheduling, adding the need to monitor the schedule. Again, the class syllabus provides checkpoints, dates for drafts and opportunities for in-class group work, so some monitoring devices are already in place. But I emphasize the need for the group to monitor its own progress. As I have already mentioned, professors might want to appoint or have the group appoint a Scheduler, a person who will keep an ongoing schedule of group deadlines and report periodically orally or in writing to the professor.

Redundancy is built into the 3 Be's because I want students to come away from the 3 Be's with a few major ideas, the primary one being the necessity of deadlines. Thus, the second and third points under Be Organized (as a Group)—complete assignments on time and counsel group members who are late to meetings and who do not understand the meaning of *dead*line—speak to deadlines. The second point is self-explanatory. The third point, however, may not be so obvious to students. I frame the third point in terms of group responsibility. "If you don't tell a group member that he or she is not acting responsibly," I say to the class, "you are endorsing the group member's behavior." I also raise issues of fairness. "If you inwardly are angry about a group member's inappropriate behavior but never voice your disapproval in civil tones, is it fair for you to critique the group member's performance negatively during the group evaluation of individual group member's performance?" Students, like most people, have a code of conduct that they use to evaluate people, and they often assume that their code is the same code everyone else uses to evaluate people. So when they are inwardly angry about a person's behavior, they assume the person has the same code they have. When I ask students to counsel group members who violate group expectations, I am doing two things. First, I am alerting groups to the need to develop guidelines for group behavior. Second, I am empowering students to enforce those rules so that nobody can later say, "But I wasn't told it was unacceptable to be late to meetings. Besides, I had to work late most of the times we had meetings." By giving students the authority to manage their groups, I hope to help them reinforce group behaviors and to provide them with a way to find out why a group member is misbehaving. If working late is the issue, the group can adjust its meeting times to accommodate the one member's scheduling problems, or the group can begin meetings at the appointed time, conduct whatever business can be conducted without the absent group member, and plan for full meetings when the group member is able to get off work and come to the meetings. In other words, students should be told to address problems as they arise—and being late to group meetings is one of those problems. And in addressing a putative problem, students may find the real problem—work schedules or babysitting arrangements.

Be Honest. The last point leads logically into Be Honest—but honesty may be a misunderstood term. Sometimes honesty is conceived as being blunt. I frame honesty not only in terms of telling the truth but also in terms of speaking politely. So when I advise group members to tell the group what they can and cannot do, I tell students to approach the truth of their talents and limitations politely. This means that a group member would not say, "I type a thousand words per minute so obviously I'll assume all word processing tasks." Rather, the group member might say, "I'm a pretty fast typist, so if I can help with word processing, I'd like to do that." Likewise, a group member should not approach a limitation, say problems with scheduling time for group meetings, by saying, "I have a very busy schedule and I can only meet outside class on Thursdays from 7 to 8 P.M." Rather, the group member might say, "Like all of you my schedule is really tight. Is it possible for us to meet on Thursdays from 7 to 8 P.M.?"

Another dimension of being honest about limitations is that a group member may not feel comfortable talking about what he or she cannot do when the group is trying to figure out what people can do. A group member might feel, "Wow! Everyone else is capable. I'd better not tell anybody what I'm not able to do." One problem with that attitude is that legitimate limitations, such as scheduling conflicts, must be addressed for the group to function efficiently. So students need to be told that being honest about limitations does not mean providing a laundry list of character deficiencies or past failures. The limitations in view are limitations that will have a negative impact on the group's performance, and such limitations need to be addressed early in the writing process.

The next point under Be Honest—express your reservations about the way the group is approaching the project—is critical. The interpersonal goal of groups is consensus, but that consensus should not be bought at the price of stifling dissensus (Mead, 1994). The purpose of consensus is effective management of the assigned writing task so that the group produces an excellent written product. Consensus does not mean that the group members have to agree about everything. It does mean that they have to agree to disagree so that disagreement does not become an irritant. The attitude cannot be, "I can forgive, but I'll never forget." Rather, through dialogue and rational arguments, the group should come to consensus about what direction to take in any given situation.

The last point under Be Honest is "counsel weak group members." Again, the 3 Be's are redundant, and rightly so. Group members need to recognize that group writing projects have enormous potential for problems and that problems, when they are detected, need to be dealt with directly and humanely. Group members who are not carrying their load need to know that they are not fooling the group and that the group is not going to let inappropriate behavior slide. To reinforce the 3 Be's, I give each student a copy of the evaluation form each group member will use to evaluate every other group member at the end of the project (Figure 6). I give the students this form at the beginning of the project not only to reinforce the behavioral standards I have outlined but also to let students know that they will be evaluated by their peers and that I will take such evaluations into account when I assign a group grade.

Consensus does not mean that the group members have to agree about everything. It does mean that they have to agree to disagree so that disagreement does not become an irritant.

At the beginning of the project, I tell the class that I will give one grade for each group project and that everyone in the group will receive that grade. I will lower an individual's grade, however, if an individual did not do the work necessary to merit the group grade. How much I lower the grade depends on the way members evaluate each other. For instance, in a group of four members, one member's level of participation might be in question because the other members give the member 2's and 3's and write vague comments like "missed a meeting or two." In such a case, I would not give the student a lower grade than the grade I gave the group. (Other professors might give a group member with consistent 2's and 3's a lower grade, by perhaps a half letter. How

FIGURE 6
Form Students Use to Evaluate Each Other

Assessment of Individual Group Member

Group Member's Name_____

Categories		Low		High	
Planning • Encourages others to participate • Offers useful criticism • Presents viable ideas	1	2	3	4
Research • Conducts primary and secondary research • Helps others conduct research • Shares research data with group in a timely manner • Analyzes data	1	2	3	4
Writing • Writes his or her share of the document, including various drafts • Does his or her share of the word processing • Provides useful peer critiques of others' writing • Helps prepare the final copy by effective editing and proofreading	1	2	3	4
Group Meetings • Attends group meetings regularly and on time • Informs group members when unable to attend a group meeting • Provides leadership in resolving conflicts • Treats all group members respectfully	1	2	3	4

Additional Comments:

much a professor reduces an individual group member's grade depends in part on grading style and philosophy. In presenting my practices, I am merely being illustrative.) If, however, the group members give 1's and 2's to one of the group members and say, "missed group meetings consistently and didn't do her part of the writing," I would have good evidence to lower that group member's grade considerably; if the group grade is a B, I might give the group member a C–.

When a group project is due, I ask each group member to provide me with an evaluation of every other group member using the form I provided at the beginning of the project. (Each group member has to make copies of the form, because I want one form for each group member.) I sort group evaluations so that I can see how everyone in the group evaluated Member A, Member B, and so on.

In using this method of evaluation, I have found that group members universally give low ratings to others who are not good group members. Very seldom do I get lukewarm evaluations. Either group members give everyone high evaluations, or they focus on one member and give him or her a low evaluation. These evaluations are generally not a surprise to me because I have been keeping in touch with the groups throughout the project, and I often have members from a group with a poorly performing member come to me and ask for advice about how to handle that member.

Thus far in this chapter, I have outlined ways that professors can help students prepare to be effective collaborators. I have provided details about preparation for collaborative writing projects, because professors should devote a significant amount of the time allocated for a collaborative writing project to preparatory needs. The last section of this chapter is therefore predicated on the proposition that maintenance or management of groups is less time-consuming than all the efforts professors exert to get groups going. Just because groups require less time for maintenance, particularly if the groups have been given excellent professorial help in the preparatory stage, does not mean that the professor can coast until the groups provide presentation copy for professors to evaluate. Rather, professors have a new type of responsibility, that of coming to class ready to address problems and give advice about the ongoing work the group is doing.

Managing Collaborative Groups

I return to George's (1984) comments about collaborative writing groups, because she makes an important point about the professor's role in managing such groups. George concludes her discussion of collaborative writing groups by affirming that the professor is the classroom leader. In fact, George notes that group work increases, instead of diminishes, the professor's responsibility in the class. Group work, according to George, "forces teachers to constantly listen, constantly watch, constantly suggest. Teachers cannot come [to class] prepared with a neatly outlined talk or a planned discussion. They must, however, come prepared to work through problems that naturally arise within the context of such a class" (p. 326). I hasten to add, however, that if professors do the preliminary work necessary to acclimate groups to collaborative writing tasks, the maintenance of groups becomes more manageable.

To discuss how professors can manage groups, I first refer to the techniques I have already mentioned. For instance, if professors choose to have students produce agendas, group minutes, and progress reports, part of managing groups is ensuring that the groups produce—on time—the documents professors requested. Professors can create their own time lines, showing which documents are due when, or they can simply ensure that the class syllabus informs students about due dates for such documents. I have found that a full-fledged collaborative project is complex for students, so I take the initiative to remind students about due dates, constantly going over the schedule so that students think ahead as they work on the project. In short, when professors start the engines that run a collaborative writing project, one dimension of managing the project is managing the forms and processes associated with the engines.

My second point is that professors will need to provide students with additional training in group interactions regarding peer review. Many students do not feel comfortable critiquing a peer's writing either because students believe that they do not have the requisite knowledge about writing to critique peers' writing effectively or because students do not want to make negative comments about their peers' work. I take these concerns as legitimate, and I believe that professors have an obligation to address these concerns to help students become effective critiquers of their peers' writing. The rest of this chapter is devoted to a discussion of how professors can train students to be effective peer critiquers by addressing the two major concerns students bring to a critique of peers' writing.

Students' Concerns About Requisite Knowledge

What students generally mean when they say, in so many words, that they are not competent to evaluate a peer's writing is that they do not know all the fine points of mechanics and grammar; they also may not have great confidence in their spelling ability. They may not know the difference between *its* and *it's* or may not detect the misuse of *their* when it is substituted for *there*. Students' focus on such points provides evidence that they have been taught that good writing is a matter of correctness. A good writer, they believe, does not make sophomoric mistakes, and anyone who is called to judge good writing would certainly have to have the knowledge to identify and correct such mistakes.

Unfortunately, many English teachers share students' mistaken notion of what constitutes good writing. I suspect, in fact, that students' conceptions of good writing have been born and bred in English classrooms throughout the United States. I will go further. I suspect that many people believe that good writing is error-free writing, including professors in higher education throughout the United States, because English teachers have been habituated to marking errors on students' papers, even to the detriment of making genuinely positive comments to encourage students to revise their writing and thus improve it, not merely correct it. (For professors interested in the history of how English teachers began focusing on correctness, see Connors, 1985.) Given the insistent declamation that good writing is error-free writing, is it not curious that even English teachers have trouble identifying errors (Connors and Lunsford, 1988; Greenbaum and Taylor, 1981) and agreeing upon what constitutes an error (Lees, 1989)? Little wonder that students are not able to articulate a standard set of rules for writing (Harris, 1997; Wall and Hull, 1989).

Unfortunately, many English teachers share students' mistaken notion of what constitutes good writing.

I remember one incident that confirms the pervasive idea that good writing equals error-free writing. When I was conducting writing-across-the-curriculum seminars, I labored to talk about *good* writing in terms of particular contexts. For instance, I noted that a good research article in chemistry is much different from a good research article in philosophy. A novel is evaluated using different criteria of goodness from a textbook on accounting. I thought I had done a thorough job of persuading a group of about twenty professors from disciplines across the curriculum that no universal definition of good writing exists because good writing depends on genre, purpose, and audience. At the end of my presentation, a professor who had been a public school teacher thanked me for my presentation, looked me straight in the eye, and said quite confidently, "I still think good writing is good writing." What my colleague meant was that good writing really is good because it is error free—and apparently context free. Little wonder that students think good writing is good because it is error-free writing. And if students subscribe to that definition of good writing, most of them really are not prepared to evaluate their peers' writing in any other way than marking errors.

But I beg to differ with the common conception that good writing is error-free writing or that good writing has some vague universal substance that makes it good. Rather, I suggest that good writing has a clear purpose and satisfies the needs of particular audiences. In other words, when professors read student writing, "the writer is granted his meanings and purposes, and is judged only on the effectiveness with which those meanings and purposes are fulfilled" (Hirsch and Harrington, 1981, p. 196). Or as Harris (1997, p. 83) says, teachers "need to respond to what students are trying to say, to the effectiveness of their writing as a whole, and not simply to the presence or absence of local errors in spelling, syntax, or usage." In fact, "excessive criticism and overemphasis on error correction and filling students' papers with red marks are NOT effective methods of feedback and do not improve the quality of student writing" (Fedje and Essex-Buss, 1989, p. 191). Professors can help students be good readers of their peers' writing by telling them to suspend for a time the need to hunt for errors and to read their peers' writing with the goal of identifying a clear purpose and determining whether that purpose meets the needs of the audience or audiences the author envisioned.

For professors to help students be good readers of peers' writing, however, professors more than likely will have to take their own advice and suspend for a time the need to find fault with students' writing (Halsted, 1974; Heffernan, 1983; Williams, 1981). Virtually all the training professors receive to become professors focuses on learning how to criticize ideas down to the last jot and tittle. The natural professorial act is to find errors of all kinds in a student's writing and measure the quality of that writing based on the student's inability to use standard written edited English. But here's the kicker: most professors do not know all the rules about standard English (who does?), so they mark a student's paper given the rules they do know, sometimes assuming that what they know is enough or what they do not know does not matter. Or perhaps professors have lingering doubts about their ability to identify errors. In writing-across-the-curriculum seminars I have conducted, professors have honestly said, "I don't remember all the technical names associated with grammar, so how can I mark students' papers. What language can I use to identify errors?" My response? "You don't need to know the technical names. You need, however, to read students' papers the same way you would read a journal article in your field. You need to read as a real reader, not a make-believe reader. You need to tell students what you, as a reader, not as a professor, think about their writing. And in doing that you need to encourage your students to keep writing." As Corder (1989) noted, when he completed the writing assignment he had assigned to his students and gave his writing to the students, "I wanted to be understood, appreciated, answered, cherished" (p. 95), not graded.

How can professors read students' texts so that students see that professors are genuinely trying to understand their texts, answering their texts from a reader's perspective, even appreciating and at times cherishing those texts? First, they can show students drafts of a piece of writing they are struggling to complete. Professors can show students examples when they themselves confused *its* and *it's*. Let students see that such errors are common. Professors can show students how they themselves struggled to get ideas down on paper, kept them from growing wild, or nurtured ideas that seemed not to be going anywhere at all. By showing students the trials and tribulations professors encounter in writing, professors can identify with the struggles students go through as they write.

Second, professors can read students' writing aloud to the class and ask the class to identify the author's thesis. If the class cannot identify a thesis, professors can ask them what the paper is about. In other words, get students to think about the paper's thesis so that they can consider purpose in writing. Many students, especially freshmen, think that stringing words together is a feat in and of itself, so they are not prepared to go the next step and determine whether their words mean anything when all the strings are put together.

Third, professors can conduct professor-student conferences in front of the class. Ask for a volunteer. Have that person (as a representative of a collaborative group) read a draft of the group's paper aloud to the class. Then ask the student questions about the paper. "What exactly did you mean when you said, 'Love is the answer to all of life's problems'? How are you defining love?" "I was very interested in your portrait of the IRS as an organization founded on illegal political maneuvers. What evidence did you provide to substantiate your claim?" "When you talk about Horowitz as one of the greatest pianists who ever lived, I kept wondering what made him so great. Can you give me details about why he was a great musician? What about his playing was so significant?" These are the types of questions readers ask, readers who are engaged in trying to understand what the writer has said, not trying to correct grammatical, mechanical, and spelling errors. Indeed, reading aloud has two virtues. First, the audience does not know whether the writer wrote *its* or *it's*, so the audience can concentrate on listening for meaning. Second, the writer finds problems because reading aloud helps unmask problems that silent reading can hide. When reading aloud, writers stumble over a particular phrase or see that a pronoun has no reference or recognize a gap between what they intended to say and what they actually wrote down.

Fourth, professors can tell students that the problem of errors will be taken care of in two ways. First, some errors will disappear as groups revise. The passage with five misspellings will not be a problem in the later drafts, because that passage will be eliminated once the group realizes that the passage does not fit with the purpose they have established for the written document they are producing. Second, errors will get fixed during the editing and proofreading stages of the composing process. Students need to know that during the early stages of the writing process, they have the liberty to write without undue concern about making mistakes. In fact, professors can tell students that errors are a natural and normal part of the writing process. Students are not expected to produce perfect copy when they create a first draft or a second draft or a third draft. After they have had the opportunity to figure out what they want and need to say, then students can begin to think about ensuring that their writing is free from surface-level errors (spelling, mechanical, and grammatical errors) that irritate readers and distract them from paying attention to the ideas the group is presenting. And professors can assure students that when the time for editing and proofreading comes, the professors will direct students to resources, such as grammar handbooks and handouts professors have developed to address persistent errors, that will help students identify and correct common errors.

If professors help students to read as real readers, not English teachers, they will be telling students that they do have the requisite knowledge to be good readers of their peers' writing. That is, students do know how to listen to a piece of writing and how to ask questions about that writing. Students do know when something does not sound right, and although they might not know immediately how to fix the problem they have identified, they can engage in a dialogue with peers to find out what the group meant to say when it penned a passage that is difficult for readers to process. In other words, in the early stages of the writing process, readers should not try to correct peers' writing. They should listen to the writing, probably using several readings, and ask questions that good readers ask, questions about clarity, meaning, purpose, and audience. Students are capable of being good readers; in fact, they can develop as readers and become astute audiences for peers' writing. The model of reading that professors present to students is the model they can use when they work in groups to review and revise their writing.

Students' Concerns About Negative Criticism

A second concern students have is that they do not want to be seen as making negative criticisms of peers' writing. Students, I have found, tend to prize friendship and goodwill among their classmates, so they are unwilling to risk making their peers angry with them. Indeed, students know what it feels like to have someone criticize their writing, and they do not want to be seen as the person who caused hurt feelings. Again, the solution to students' fear of being the messenger of negative criticism is to show students how to make positive comments about peers' writing and how to offer suggestions from a reader's viewpoint about ways to improve the writing.

Provide students with opportunities to write without the fear of offending authors. Brown (1984), for instance, brings the writing of published authors to class and asks students to evaluate it. She says that students are more likely to make useful critiques about such writing because they do not fear offending the authors. Professors can achieve the same critical distance by having students analyze writing from students in previous classes (with the student writers' permission to use the writing). I have found that using examples of both effective and ineffective writing from previous students the present class does not know helps students see the contrast between effective and ineffective writing. For example, after students analyze the features of a well written resume from an anonymous student in a previous class, they have standards to use when evaluating a poorly written resume from another anonymous student in a previous class, and they can see why the poorly written resume is faulty.

Require authors to read their writing and listen without responding to peer critiquers. Authors (or a representative author from a collaborative group) can read their writing to a peer group, listen to the group's responses without making comments, and when all the comments have been made, ask questions for clarification only. The purpose of this approach is to focus on comments and not allow the author an opportunity to defend his/her/their writing. This approach also assumes that authors have the authority to reject or to accept peer responses when revising their writing, so authors do not need to defend their writing in the face of suggestions for revision.

Teach students to make positive comments. Literature on teachers' responses to student writing notes that teachers do not have a good record of responding positively to student writing (Connors and Lunsford, 1993; Daiker, 1989; Gee, 1972; Lamberg, 1977). Because teachers model for students how to respond to writing, it is likely that students will have limited ways to respond positively to peers' writing. (By *respond positively,* I do not mean student responses such as "Hey! Good job!") The literature on peer response both recognizes the need to teach students to respond positively to peers' writing and offers suggestions for making positive responses. Hays (1982), for example, tells students, "Find three places where the writer . . . has done a good job of developing a point . . . " (p. 117). Neubert and McNelis (1990) recommend the PQP method—Praise-Question-Polish— noting that praise is rightly the first obligation of a peer reviewer. This point needs to be emphasized for two reasons. One, it makes good sense on an interpersonal level to point out what works with a piece of writing first. The peer reviewer is sending a signal to the writer that whatever recommendations the peer reviewer is making are based on goodwill. Two, a major purpose of peer review is to help writers revise. As Harris (1992) notes, peer review is designed to strengthen students' critical-thinking skills and sense of audience, and praise is a major incentive for motivating students to think critically and consider audience carefully. In response to praise, a writer might think, "She liked what I said and is helping me make it better." Attitude is central to the peer review enterprise, and peer reviewers with positive attitudes about their role as helpers can be more effective than peer reviewers (including professors) who see themselves as judges. By championing a positive attitude in peer review, I am not suggesting that students say nice things for the sake of saying nice things to ingratiate themselves with authors. Rather, I am saying that writers need and deserve praise for writing because writing is a demanding activity that exposes the author to intellectual challenge. Praise for what the author did well is essential in giving authors balanced comments about their writing.

Teach students to make specific comments. Hayes and Daiker (1984) say that the purpose of commenting on students' writing is to show students what options they have as writers. To show students options, peer critiquers need to make specific comments (Cannon, 1989; Grimm, 1986). Comments such as "Good job!" or "This piece has real problems" are not helpful in providing students with information about how to revise their writing. What specifically, from the audience's point of view, needs to be clarified, developed, deleted, or defined? Professors can use various strategies (see, e.g., Elbow and Belanoff, 1989; Gere, 1982; Holt, 1992; Spear, 1988) to help students make specific comments. Professors will need to reinforce again and again the need for students to make specific comments, because students tend to focus on generalities in responding to student writing. In addition, professors can help writers ask questions to elicit specific comments (Danis, 1982).

Teach students to focus on one or two major points for revision. Literature on teachers' responses to students' writing points out that teachers can sometimes mark a student's paper so much that the student has no idea where to begin addressing all the problems the teacher has identified (Lamberg, 1980). Professors should teach students not to make the same mistake. Thus, professors can explain to students that the purpose of peer review in the early stages of the writing process is to help writers achieve greater focus with the writing, not to correct errors. Peer reviewers can help peers achieve greater focus by stressing one or two major suggestions for revision. For instance, a peer reviewer could say, "As a reader, I'm not sure how your third section fits with your second section. What are you saying about the relationship between inflation and interest rates?" Such a comment might enable the writer to ask more questions about the reader's concern or to explain the relationship. In explaining the relationship, the peer reviewer has the opportunity to ask for more points of clarification to help determine what is hindering the reader from making the connection between inflation and interest rates that the writer is trying to make.

Teach students not to compensate for gaps in peers' writing. Flynn (1982) says that students often compensate for a writer's inability to express ideas clearly. Students, for instance, will fill in gaps of information. The antidote to this malady is to teach students to read critically, to ask questions that they are not accustomed to asking about writing. Professors can model asking such questions by reading a piece of writing in front of the class and making comments about gaps in the writing so that students begin to see that they need to enlarge their storehouse of peer review questioning techniques.

Provide students with forms for critiquing peers' writing. Flynn (1982) recommends that professors provide students with peer critique sheets to help them see what kinds of questions to ask. Figure 2 in Chapter 3 is an example of a peer critique sheet, but other examples are available—Brumback, 1985; Folks, 1979; Messelaar, 1976; Meyers, 1988; Pianko and Radzik, 1980).

Assign critiquing roles to group members. Meyers (1989) recommends that each member of a group be assigned a specific writing trait (i.e., format, organization, style, precision, audience considerations) as the sole focus of his or her feedback. This suggestion has merit, particularly when students provide peer critiques later in the writing process after writers have been able to shape and structure their writing to satisfy purpose and audience requirements and are ready to tighten the document. Another possibility in assigning roles to the group is for professors to ask one person in the group to ensure that everyone responds to the writing. This approach ensures that all members of the group have the opportunity (and see the obligation) to make positive responses that will improve the document under consideration.

Meet with groups early in the writing process to model helpful critiquing behaviors. Professors can meet with groups early in the writing process to model the types of responses listed above. In fact, Walvoord (1986) recommends that professors scatter group meetings so that they can meet with each group to model effective response.

Use recordings of groups' peer critiques to train students in critiquing methods. Professors can videotape groups involved in peer critiquing and use the videotape to help students analyze effective and ineffective critique methods. Benesch (1984) also recommends that professors audiotape peer response sessions, make a transcript of the audiotape, and ask students to analyze the transcript to find ways to improve their responses.

Differentiate revising from editing and proofreading. I noted previously that the early stages of peer critiquing should focus on one or two ways that authors can revise their texts. I emphasize the distinction between revising and editing/proofreading, because professors need to make students aware of the distinction. According to research that Nystrand (1986) conducted, students tended to see peer review as mere editing unless they were part of the writing studio groups. Students in such groups learned to see peer review as a means for revising effectively. Editing, the process used in the final stages of the writing process to detect and fix surface errors and make final recommendations about style, organization, and content, is a vital part of the writing process and should be included late in the peer review process. But editing should be seen as separate from revising. In fact, Sommers (1982) says that teachers confuse students by giving advice to revise and edit at the same time. Revising, as I have been discussing it, focuses on global issues related to genre, purpose, and audience, narrowing over time to editing advice about more detailed and specific needs. Frankly, I do not know where revising ends and editing begins, but I do know that professors need to distinguish between the two so that students focus on revision in the early stages of the writing process.

In all that I have said about peer evaluation, I have assumed that the professor will take the following advice about responding to student writing: that the professor can respond to student writing using four types of responses (respond, judge, analyze, and improve) and that good professors adopt a particular type of response "depending on the stage at which the composition is read" (Purves, 1984, p. 263). Virtually everything I have said about students' role as peer reviewers applies to professors' role as responders to student writing and vice versa. That is, the type of response (whether the responder is a student or a professor) depends on the stage of the writing process. Early in the process, students (and professors) need to be taught to be positive, encouraging peers to continue writing, and to be helpful in suggesting to peers how to hone their thesis and support it. As the writing process evolves, students (and professors) can provide more specific comments about the writing, more analysis. Even later, students (and professors) can begin to make judgments about the quality of the writing, albeit judgments in keeping with the goal of formative evaluation—to help writers be highly successful when their documents are scrutinized during summative evaluation. Toward the end of the writing process, peers can help peers focus on all the nitty-gritty details of preparing a manuscript for publication: crossing t's, dotting i's, pointing out mistakes in spelling that continue to linger, identifying sentences that are too long and cause readers to get lost, suggesting the need for a bit more detail, recommending that a restructuring of a particular passage might provide a more logical route to an idea—keeping in mind that in all the stages of peer review during the concomitant stages of the writing process, the goal is to help writers be successful.

Conclusion

I agree with Holt's (1992) statement that "No one's version of collaborative pedagogy is universally rewarding, of course, but I have found some approaches consistently more successful than others" (p. 384). I add, however, that the collaborative classroom is dynamic, so professors need choices as they consider which pedagogical methods might work best for them. Thus, this chapter has provided a catalogue of ways that professors can approach forming collaborative groups, training students to be effective collaborators, and managing collaborative groups effectively. In providing choices, I recognize that professors might wonder what their obligation is in using various techniques to help students learn successful collaboration. I would be presumptuous to answer that question for professors in particular classrooms. Others, however, have provided advice about collaborative writing in particular disciplines, including business communication (e.g., Baker, 1986; Belanger and Greer, 1992; Forman, 1989; Knodt, 1994; Merrier, 1988; Renshaw, 1990), journalism (e.g., Bissland, 1980; Irby, 1995), literature (e.g., Brown-Guillory, 1987; Young, 1994), philosophy (Bosley and Jacobs, 1992), mathematics (Carton, 1990), and history (Steffens, 1989), and the information in this chapter should provide a reliable road map for professors as they seek to promote collaborative writing in their particular situations.

Collaborative Writing and Computers

HYPERTEXT. Computer-mediated classrooms. Groupware. Asynchronous. LAN. CAI. Networked microcomputer classroom. Shareware. Electronic bulletin boards. Workstations. Hardware. Software. Synchronous. File server. Writing lab. Streaming video. Electronic mail. Computer conferencing. File access.

Welcome to the literature on collaborative writing and computers! The terms above are commonly used in that literature, yet professors may not be familiar with them or not familiar enough to readily define each term. Therefore, one of the first challenges for professors in investigating collaborative writing in relationship to computer technology is the very language used to talk about that relationship. This chapter provides a nontechnical discussion of collaborative writing and computer technology to address two fundamental issues. Why should professors consider using computer technology to teach collaborative writing? And what problems might professors encounter when they teach collaborative writing using computer technology?

Why Use Computer Technology to Teach Collaborative Writing?

Enthusiasts of computer technology would probably stare in wonder that anyone would ask why professors should consider using computer technology to teach collaborative writing. After all, computers exist! And, it appears, computers not only are ubiquitous but also rule most of life's day-to-day transactions. Not to use computers in teaching, enthusiasts likely would respond, is unthinkable. Without engaging in a protracted debate about the value of computers in the classroom, I do think that computer technology is so pervasive that only Luddites will argue against any use of computers in the classroom. So I acknowledge as valid the point that market forces combined with technological innovation have changed in some ways the "delivery" of education. But I take a cautious approach, subscribing to Hacker and Niederhauser's (2000) statement that "it would be remiss for advocates of online learning to promote it on the basis of expediency and not on quality" (p. 53). In fact, later in this chapter I cite issues professors will want to consider when they evaluate the pros and cons not only of on-line courses but also of integrating computer technology in collaborative writing projects.

When we speak of computer technology, we are using a plastic moniker, not a monolithic concept. Indeed, the choices for both the capabilities of computers and the programs for those computers are staggering—and protean. A constant flow of new products (and upgrades) makes obsolete the products computer users have come to rely on. So questions about availability of a particular computer technology depend on market forces that promote sales, not stability. For instance, the computer program a professor uses this academic year to teach an on-line course may not be available next year because of changes in licensing agreements or price considerations from competitors who market rival programs. In general, however, computer technology can be discussed under two major components: facilities and programs.

Under facilities, I include what is commonly called *hardware,* the computer itself and the immediate environment that houses the hardware, from a single workstation, the physical location of the computer, to a room designed for multiple computers. Thus, facilities can be characterized as one computer, more than one computer, or computer laboratories.

The second component of computer technology is programs, commonly called *software* or the brains in the computer body. As brains (and there are multiple brains because of multiple software packages), the programs allow users to tell the computer what to do. What kinds of programs are available? I classify programs under two types: programs whose primary purpose is to allow a user to create text and programs that enable users to interact with each other using more than one computer. Word processing programs, desktop publishing programs, and hypertext programs are examples of the first type, although hypertext programs can include dimensions of the second type. Under the second type are electronic bulletin boards, chat rooms, e-mail, and specific programs that allow students to interact with each other electronically when discussing texts, such as *Interchange, Comments, Talk, Colab* (Duin and Hansen, 1994). These programs can aid students in creating presentation copy by enabling them to critique peers' work, to communicate about scheduling the work, and to discuss other issues related to the task of creating a document. Certainly, I have given a very broad view of programs, and others could make finer distinctions. My purpose in giving a broad view is to relate programs specifically to the pedagogy of collaborative writing.

The bulk of literature on collaborative writing and computer technology assumes some sort of computer laboratory, generally one where the computers are linked together by programs (networked) so that students can communicate with each other using the computers. Many of the following comments about the usefulness of computer technology in promoting collaborative writing assume a networked computer environment. In principle, however, proponents of linking collaborative writing and computer technology often acknowledge that even a single computer in the classroom can foster a greater sense of collaboration among students than no computer at all.

Computer technology supports the writing process by making brainstorming, writing, revising, and editing easier (Arms, 1983, 1985). Cornell and Newton (1988) compared the writing of students who worked together using computers and those who did not. They found that the computer group tended to suggest more global revisions than did the control group. Cyganowski (1990) says that computers help students talk about writing as a recursive, not linear, process. Kinkead (1988) notes that computer networks enhanced peer review, allowed mentors to respond to student writing, and allowed students to maintain a running dialogue on texts, all ways to support the writing process. Neuwirth and Wojahn (1996) agree that computers are useful in peer critiques, and Rada, Michailidis, and Wang (1994) found in their study of collaborative hypermedia technology that "people who make comments of substance on their partners' work are more likely to improve their performance as compared with their performance when they write alone" (p. 34). Van Pelt and Gillam (1991) assert that computers facilitate communication among group members, particularly in the exchange of drafts or feedback on-line. Skubikowski and Elder (1990) go so far as to say that the success their students experienced in a networked computer lab can be attributed to "the energy, commitment, and collaboration generated on the network" (p. 93). Thus, computer technology can enable students to create higher-quality documents than they would without computer technology (Bernhardt and Appleby, 1985).

Computer technology can heighten students' sense of audience (Sudol, 1985). When students create hypertexts, for instance, considerations regarding audience are intensified. A hypertext itself is not designed to be read from cover to cover but to allow multiple points of entry so that readers can make many choices about what they want to view and in what order. Davis (1991), in discussing his students' experiences creating hypertexts collaboratively, notes that students "must consider many more possible relationships among pieces of information, and they must consider many more possible reader paths through that information" (p. 144). But even a networked classroom without the use of hypertext has the potential to give more students in the class an opportunity to review one student's writing, especially when that student's writing is posted to an electronic bulletin board where classmates can read it and respond to it via computer.

Computer technology has the potential to encourage students who might not participate very much to participate in collaborative projects (Langston and Batson, 1990; Selfe, 1992; Yeoman, 1995). Faigley (1990) notes that network discussions serve an equalizing function; students who might be reluctant to speak usually have no problem participating via computer. Kowalski (1989) discusses a particular computer program and says one of its benefits is that students who might be reluctant to speak up in class have no difficulty collaborating using the program. Kiesler, Siegel, and McGuire (1984) confirm Kowalski's observation when they note that in their study, participants in a computer-mediated group were less inhibited than those in the face-to-face group.

Computer technology promotes the learning-centered classroom by providing students with new opportunities to take responsibility for their learning and for professors to assume the coaching role (Batson, 1988; Duin, Jorn, and DeBower, 1991; Eldred, 1989; Langston and Batson, 1990). According to Reynolds (1988), even the physical layout of a computer lab can encourage greater interaction among students. Reynolds found that a significant amount of collaboration occurred around tables, desks, bulletin boards, and file cabinets. Thus, the overriding principle for computer lab design is to facilitate communication. Selfe and Wahlstrom (1985) support this viewpoint when they note that a computer lab encourages collaboration by providing a common physical space for writers to work together. Coppola (1996) noted the value of "active dialogue and sense of camaraderie that developed among the students as they solved problems, formed groups, and collaborated on assignments" (p. 42).

Computer technology can help both group members and the professor manage a collaborative project more efficiently. For instance, Min and Rada (1994) and Fish, Kraut, Leland, and Cohen (1988) discuss computer programs that allow collaborators to keep track of the group's writing activities.

What Problems Might Arise in Using Computer Technology to Teach Collaborative Writing?

Computer technology, for all its potential to promote collaborative writing, is not without problems, and professors should be aware of difficulties they might encounter as they use computer technology to help students write collaboratively. Two broad problems can occur when professors use computer technology: those related to technical support and those related to pedagogical issues.

Technical Support

When professors link their teaching inextricably to a particular technology, whether chalkboards or computers, they become dependent on that technology.

This dependence becomes particularly evident when the technology fails. Without chalk, using the chalkboard as a way to provide information to students becomes very difficult. When certain technologies, however, fail to provide the medium for instruction, professors can go to a fallback position and use, say, dictation in lieu of writing instructions on the chalkboard. Computer technology makes such fallback positions much more difficult. A PowerPoint presentation is qualitatively different from an oral presentation that shows slides on an overhead made from the PowerPoint presentation. When professors depend on PowerPoint to give a presentation to students but are unable to do so because of technical glitches, the fallback position is less attractive. Thus, the instability of computer technology at various points—obsolescence of particular programs, compatibility issues among programs, technical failures during presentations—should give professors pause as they consider how heavily to invest their curricular materials in computer technology.

Another issue related to technical support is the actual support a campus provides for the pedagogical use of computer technology. When technological glitches occur, professors want to be assured that they will be fixed quickly. Does the college or university have adequate technical personnel and necessary equipment to support the professor's use of computer technology in the classroom? Schwartz and Froehlke (1990), for instance, note that barriers to using computers in education include high costs and conflicts among various units on a campus. High costs include the costs for support personnel, and such personnel are in demand, so their salaries are competitive with industry standards, not standards in the academy. Conflicts among various units on a campus include conflicts between those in charge of technology and those who are supported by those in charge. Unfortunately, the attitude of those in charge might be condescending because those who are served are not techies, people who speak the language of those in charge. The friction between those in charge and those served by those in charge can have major negative implications for the use of computer technology to support collaborative writing in the classroom. In fact, Haas and Neuwirth (1994) raise significant questions about the assumptions professors may make about technology, showing that unless professors are actively engaged in the decision-making process concerning computer use and are actively conducting research about how computers do or do not promote literacy, professors will forfeit the opportunity to shape technological use in the academy.

Configuration of computer labs can be a problem (Gerson, 1993). Computer labs can have a major positive influence on collaboration, not only in terms of the programs used to promote collaborative writing but also in terms of the design of those labs. If computer labs are designed without input from those who will use them to teach collaborative writing or others knowledgeable about pedagogical requirements for computer labs, a lab could be a great hindrance to teaching students effective collaborative writing using computers.

Whether classrooms are wired for technology and how many classrooms are wired also affect professors' ability to use computer technology. Professors can be frustrated easily in their use of technology when they transport computer equipment to a classroom that is not wired for technological use. Or a wired classroom may be assigned to a professor who does not use technology while the professor who does use technology is assigned a classroom that is not wired. Administrators who promote the use of technology in the classroom must, to make their rhetoric more than sweet words for public consumption, provide the necessary resources; they must also ensure that wired rooms are assigned to the professors who need them.

All these technical problems can have an additional dimension when professors have little say about how technology is developed, purchased, and used. In other words, professors "should not assume that literacy *technologies* are either straightforward or unproblematic. Views of computers, like views of literacy, are value-laden. Conceptions of what technology *is,* and how it comes to be, profoundly shape specific acts of computer-based reading and writing" (Haas and Neuwirth, 1994, p. 319). Professors should have an active role in decisions about what technology is used and how it is used in teaching students how to write collaboratively, because the ways technological products are created and used are linked to philosophies about literacy, about how to read and write effectively.

Pedagogical Issues

Lack of face-to-face interaction can hinder collaborative writing. Johnson and Johnson (1986) note that computers do not promote the oral exchange of information that has been shown to be necessary for cognitive development. In addition, they assert that the feedback students receive orally in groups has more impact than feedback via computer. Kaye (1993), in supporting the use of computers to teach collaborative writing, nevertheless says that successful computer collaboration requires face-to-face communication. Newman and Newman (1993) say that collaborative writing with the support of a computer often suffers because communication via computer lacks many of the essential cues of face-to-face communication. E-mail, for instance, lacks certain communication cues, such as facial gestures, and because of the impersonal nature of e-mail, those who send such messages may send inappropriate comments because e-mail offers few social inhibitions (Sproull and Kiesler, 1986). In other words, computer technology may enforce antisocial behaviors. In addition, Galegher and Kraut (1990), Handa (1990), and Kearsley (1988) note that hypertext projects can create problems because of the lack of face-to-face communication among group members. Charney (1994) even raises questions about hypertext as an appropriate way to promote reading and writing, because assumptions on which hypertext are based "contradict current thinking in rhetorical theory, cognitive psychology, and document design" (p. 241). Hartley (1984), although affirming that computer "programs are more thorough and systematic" (p. 43) than humans are when writing is being evaluated for grammatical, mechanical, and spelling consistency, cautions that computer programs cannot tell whether a piece of writing is publishable. Therefore, Hartley recommends both peer feedback and computer-assisted editing. Computer technology alone does not humanize writing; it merely facilitates the writing process and cannot completely facilitate the process, because face-to-face contact is still needed.

Computer technology can subvert the learning-centered classroom. Hawisher and Selfe (1991) note that electronic bulletin boards can become a device for reinforcing professorial authority rather than enabling collaboration. One of the hopes of collaborative writing to disperse authority among students and the professor therefore can be subverted. Selfe and Eilola (1988), in their study of interaction among participants in a computer network, found that network collaboration is not as egalitarian as has been assumed, even when participants use pseudonyms to mask their status. Their study is another indication that the hope for increased participation by members of the class who may not have felt comfortable participating openly in traditional classrooms can be subverted by the use of computer technology. In addition, networked classrooms may not be user-friendly for students, so such classrooms may hinder the learning process (Hawisher, 1992). Noting that professors face a number of challenges in creating a useful computer lab to support collaborative writing, Selfe (1987) provides advice about how to create a useful lab.

Professors may lack training in computer technology. In addition to the managing and training discussed earlier, professors need to become conversant with computer technology so they can train students how to use that technology effectively during collaborative writing projects. Forman (1990) says that teachers should instruct students about group dynamics, about the efficient use of the technology, and about effective methods for managing writing tasks and using technology. Indeed, "unexamined additions of technology to the collaborative classroom can, in fact, intensify the difficulties of teaching and learning" (Forman, 1994, p. 131). Kemp (1993) and Sullivan (1994) agree that professors must become skilled in the use of computer technology to train students how to collaborate effectively in computer classrooms. Thus, professors can add yet another requirement to their job descriptions, and because of the instability of computer technology, the training, both for professors and students, will be ongoing.

Conclusion

This chapter has not provided techniques for using computer technology to promote collaborative writing, because specific techniques depend on the particular facilities and programs available to each professor. The principles throughout this volume concerning the pedagogy of collaborative writing, according to much of the literature cited in this chapter, however, fit with the use of computer technology. That professors are using computer technology effectively to teach collaborative writing is beyond question. That computer technology is the best option for teaching collaborative writing remains an open question. Part of the reason that professors cannot speak with absolute authority about how effective technology will be in promoting literacy is that "few of us are equipped to function effectively and comfortably in virtual literacy environments. Indeed, like many citizens, college faculty are just beginning to learn what it means to work successfully within a society that is dependent on computer technology for literacy activities. We are only beginning to identify, for example, the complexity of the challenges posed by such a society, including the challenge of adapting to an increasingly rapid pace of change. Nor do we necessarily have the lived experiences that allow us to deal productively with this climate of change" (Hawisher and Selfe, 1999, p. 3).

> **That professors are using computer technology effectively to teach collaborative writing is beyond question. That computer technology is the best option for teaching collaborative writing remains an open question.**

Therefore, I return to Hacker and Niederhauser (2000), who express a cautious optimism about the use of on-line courses. Their observations about on-line courses are germane to the subject of collaborative writing and computer technology, because an on-line course really is, at present, the supreme example of wedding computer technology and writing pedagogy; students communicate solely through writing, and their writing is public most of the time. Hacker and Niederhauser, after noting that on-line classrooms may prove even more effective than traditional classrooms, say, "Still, an important question that continually must be kept in mind is whether the online classroom hinders learning. If the answer to this question is yes, then we must take a step back and seriously investigate what we are advocating" (p. 61). Until the academy has a larger body of data about the usefulness of on-line classes and computer technology to support learning in collaborative writing, professors might consider small doses of computer technology to teach collaborative writing and increase the dosage as professors see positive results in student learning.

Grading Students' Collaborative Writing Projects

THIS MONOGRAPH has provided ways for professors and students to be engaged in evaluating collaborative writing products and processes during the writing endeavor. Such evaluation is called *formative evaluation.* Now I address the second form of evaluation, *summative evaluation.* Both formative and summative evaluation overlap and depend on each other, so all that I have said in the previous chapters about evaluating leads to and is intertwined with what I say in this chapter about summative evaluation. To discuss summative evaluation, I address fairness and professional judgment, the problem of cheating, rubrics, and methods of assigning grades. (For professors interested in an extended treatment of grading writing, see Speck, 2000.)

Fairness

The power structure of the classroom is such that professors possess virtually all the formal authority and power. Professors have the authority to determine what materials students will be assigned; how the day-to-day class activities will be managed; how much students will be allowed to participate in the class by asking questions, engaging in group activities, and voicing their opinions about class management issues; how and when students will be evaluated; and who conducts the evaluations. Professors are very powerful people, and the checks and balances on their power are slight. Beyond generic institutional rules and guidelines about professorial behavior in the class, professors are not encumbered by explicit standards that require them to use their power in ways that help students learn. The lack of such explicit standards is probably derived from the belief that professors are professionals and should know how to use their power in the interest of student learning. Indeed, the lack of explicit standards beyond generic institutional rules and guidelines puts the onus for the rightful use of power on professors' shoulders. As professionals, professors have the responsibility to use their power wisely in the interests of promoting effective student learning.

I argued in the first chapter that professors can use their authority responsibly by engaging students in collaborative writing projects of various sorts, because collaborative writing, a subset of collaborative learning, has the potential to put the burden of learning on students' shoulders. Students are put in a position to assume authority as writers to make critical decisions about writing quality. Students also are asked to make decisions and to take responsibility by working effectively with others. And students are given the guidance they need to make responsible decisions. When professors give students such guidance, professors are using their authority and power responsibly so that students can be active learners, those who assume both authority and responsibility for their education. Thus, when professors delegate responsibility and give students the tools they need to be responsible in their use of authority, professors are equalizing the power structure of the classroom. In equalizing that power structure, I contend that professors are promoting a fair classroom.

The word *fair* is abstract, so a person could argue that fairness is a matter of one's perspective. Although I agree that fairness certainly does depend, in part, on a person's particular vantage point, I suggest that fairness must be grounded in more than perception. It must be grounded in the responsible use of power. In terms of evaluation of collaborative writing, fairness is grounded in the professor's inclusion of students in the evaluative decision-making process. I consider the inclusion of students in that process as fair, because the thrust of education is to prepare students to use knowledge in the service of the public good. Students cannot become effective evaluators of writing by merely being passive recipients of the results of professors' evaluations. When a student receives a paper that has been evaluated by a professor, professors should not assume that the student has the ability to unravel the process the professor used to make that evaluation. In fact, literature on the grading of student writing suggests that students not only evaluate writing using different criteria from those professors use but also misinterpret the criteria professors say that they use in evaluating writing (Newkirk, 1984a, 1984b). Yet the mismatch between students' perceptions of criteria for evaluating writing and professors' perceptions should not be surprising—if professors have not taken the time to explain how and why they evaluate the way they do. In other words, when professors assume that students interpret evaluative criteria the way professors interpret that criteria and then downgrade students for their misapplication of the criteria (as witnessed by low-quality writing projects), professors are not being fair. They are abusing their power, and students generally have little recourse to such abuses of professorial power, which makes the professorial abuse doubly unfair. How can this double jeopardy be changed to equitable—that is, fair—treatment of students?

First, as I have stressed throughout this volume, professors need to delegate authority so that students do have opportunities to learn how to evaluate writing effectively. One implication of this statement in terms of summative evaluation is that professors can include students in determining the grade for a collaborative project.

Second, professors need to promote the intertwining of the entire writing process and evaluation. Evaluation does not begin when professors collect final drafts and begin the laborious task of marking those drafts to arrive at a grade. Evaluation begins with the writing assignment, because in that assignment professors provide students with criteria the professor will use to arrive at a summative assessment.

Third, professors need to manage the writing process so that evaluation is intertwined with it. Thus, professors need to use peer critiques, formal and informal professor-student conferences, in-class examination of representative papers, and so on so that students learn to apply the evaluative criteria to writing.

Fourth, professors need to unveil some of the mysteries of professional judgment while maintaining the irreducible mystery of professional judgment (Speck, 1998c). In other words, professors can provide students with opportunities to understand how professional judgment operates, what criteria can be applied, and how decisions about quality are made and in these ways show students that summative evaluation is not the mystery they thought it was. At the same time, professors must maintain that experience, taste, and talent to judge are part of the evaluative mix and are not capable of being reduced to neat categories. Much of the evaluative process can be examined, taught, and replicated, but part of that process remains mysterious, because professional judgment depends on the unique capabilities of particular judges.

The Problem of Cheating

Both students and professors often consider cheating a significant problem in collaborative writing projects. The problem of cheating in collaborative writing projects is really a problem of assessment, because the central issue concerning cheating, for students, is how to get the grade they deserve and, for professors, how to give individual students in a collaborative group the grade he or she deserves. The problem of cheating has two parts.

The first part is an ethical question about collaboration. "In principle," a person might ask, "isn't collaboration a form of cheating because individual work cannot be separated?" At the foundation of this question is a view of individualistic effort as the supreme effort. If a person does not do his or her work, he or she is cheating somehow. This view of work fits well with the practices of education. Students are tested individually, and in high-stakes tests (such as the SAT) multiple safeguards are put in place to ensure that the Jerome Neggled who signed up for the test is the same Jerome Neggled who took the test. That way the Jerome Neggled who received a very high score for the test is the same Jerome Neggled who was offered a scholarship to a prestigious university. Admissions officials at such universities say, "Jerome Neggled, as an individual, is the person we want to attend our institution. We're not offering a scholarship to his parents [who helped him with his math homework], his buddy [who explained a particularly difficult concept in physics so that Jerome could understand it], or his teachers [who evidently had little to do with Jerome's academic success]. We're offering the scholarship to JEROME." Obviously, Jerome has very clear boundaries as a person, and the relationship between Jerome and all those who advised, supported, encouraged, taught, and admonished him is not acknowledged. In the end,

Jerome alone is responsible for his success. And Jerome's scores on educational tests prove that Jerome has the ability to be independently successful in other educational endeavors.

Certainly I do not believe what you have just read, and most people would find qualms with my stress on Jerome's independence. Even people who give scholarships to people like Jerome would say that Jerome's background (his home, school, and social life) had a demonstrable impact on Jerome's test scores. And I have never heard anyone say that a person like Jerome was cheating when he got "legitimate" help with his academic studies. If, however, Jerome violated academic standards, such as using unauthorized notes during an examination, virtually everyone would accuse Jerome of cheating. So it only stands to reason that when Jerome works in a group and is expected to be a team player in the group, he is not able to demonstrate individual achievement completely distinguished from group achievement. Jerome as an individual is somehow swallowed up in the group, and Jerome's reward for being able to perform as an individual is confused with the group's reward for the group's performance. For some, this swallowing of the individual into the group is an ethical dilemma, because they stress individualism at the expense of cooperation.

My response to this supposed ethical dilemma is twofold. First, the dilemma as I have stated it is imbalanced. Although groups comprise individuals, they are more than individuals. To stress individualism in group work is to negate group integrity. Just as Jerome did not lose his identity when his parents helped him with the math homework, so Jerome remains an individual in a group—but to be successful in the group, he needs to be part of the group. To stress Jerome's individuality at the expense of group integrity is to say, in essence, that individuals are better than groups, which is an absurd statement when you consider biologically how humans are created. Nevertheless, those who raise questions about the relationship between individual and group identity help us focus on an issue that is important. How fair is it for individuals like Jerome to suffer because the group of which Jerome is a member produces poor quality documents? Conversely, how fair is it for Jerome and others in the group to carry the deadweight of a group member who is not pulling his or her share of the load?

The second part of the issue of cheating is a practical question about assessment of effort, and I submit that this practical question is not entirely separable from the first part of the issue about cheating; indeed, it is part and parcel of everyday life. The second part is really an attempt to deal with the ethical perspective of the first part. That is, if professors should prize individual effort over group effort, how can they reward individual effort? The assumption of both parts of the cheating issue is that the individual is primary, the group secondary. As I show momentarily, professors have developed grading schemes based on the perceived need to reward both individuals and groups.

Ultimately, however, I think that the ethical dilemma of collaboration is so pervasive in our culture that a proposal to separate individuals within groups from the groups themselves reflects a cultural schizophrenia. In our culture, individualism is prized, and slogans such as "be all you can be" capture the spirit of individualism that so pervades the thinking of Americans. At the same time, insufficient attention is paid to the extensive support any one person needs to achieve success in most of life's endeavors. In the movie industry, the stars' names are blazoned on the theater's marquee, and not until the end of the movie when all the film credits are given does the audience, on its way out of the theater, realize how many hands were needed to put so few in the limelight. Likewise, the president of a university could not possibly do his or her job if janitors, maintenance people, professors, students, administrators of various stripes, and secretaries did not do their jobs. The examples of complex support systems that are needed for a person of prominence to achieve and maintain that position of prominence are legion. We in this country really have a false notion of individuality in that our notion is often divorced from the reality of work in everyday life. A piano tuner can have a tremendous impact on the quality of a concert pianist's performance, but most people in this country think in concert pianist categories, with little regard for the categories of piano tuner, piano maker, piano seller, and piano mover—all of which have significant implications for piano players.

Frankly, the relationship of individual to group and group to individual is complex. My purpose in discussing these relationships and the issue of cheating that is often raised in relationship to collaborative writing is to suggest that fairness is not served well when group-individual relationships are seen from an imbalanced perspective. I tend to hold to the integrity of the group, and in teaching collaborative writing, my priority is to help the group create a document that will represent the group, not individuals in the group—which does not mean that traces in the document (for instance, graphics produced by a particularly gifted student) should not bring particular attention to an individual's efforts. It does mean, however, that the group project as a whole is the focus of summative evaluation, and if the group has marshaled its resources well to produce a document that has a clear purpose and is persuasive for the specified audience, no one has cheated anyone else in the group. If an individual or individuals in the group did not pull their weight in creating the document, however, they do not deserve full credit for the document. They cheated both themselves and the group, and they should be held accountable for their lack of responsibility. Is that not a fair distinction to make between individual and group responsibility?

Rubrics

As noted, fairness in evaluation requires that professors make explicit at the beginning of the collaborative writing assignment the criteria that will be used for summative evaluation. Those same criteria should be used to evaluate the project as it is developed during the writing process, so students should have access to the criteria at the outset of the project. A rubric, a scoring guide that clearly delineates criteria and corresponding rating values to evaluate students' performance, is an excellent way to provide students with evaluative criteria. The example in Figure 7 is a modified version of a rubric I presented to a writing class.

I have just noted that professors should make evaluative criteria clear at the outset of a writing project; however, I also think it necessary for professors to allow students to be involved in establishing evaluative criteria, so I take the liberty of waiting until the first draft of a project is due to engage students in revising a rubric I provide when I introduce the assignment. I ask students to help me modify the rubric for three reasons. One, I want students to consider what really counts when their writing undergoes summative evaluation. The sample rubric I give them has categories similar to the categories

FIGURE 7
Sample Rubric for a Collaborative Writing Assignment

Categories/Point Value	Evaluations		
	Self	Peer	Teacher

Organization—25 Points (circle points of weakness)

- Theme is clearly stated and developed.

- Text of paper flows.

Content—45 Points (circle points of weakness)

- Reader understands both sides of the issue because the authors provide adequate details.

- Reader has a greater appreciation of the complexity of the issue than he or she did before reading the paper.

- Reader fully understands the issue after reading the paper and has no questions about the issue.

- Paper has required number of sources.

- Sources are used effectively.

Usage/Mechanics—30 Points (circle points of weakness)

- Authors use correct grammar.

- Paper has no run-ons or comma splices.

- Authors can use fragments if they are clearly understood to be intentional.

- Punctuation is correct.

- Capitalization is correct.

- Spelling is correct.

- Sources are cited correctly (either MLA or APA format).

Comments:

listed in Figure 7, but I ask them to give me insights about whether the categories are adequate (should one or two be eliminated or another category added), whether the descriptions of the categories are adequate, and whether the point value for each category needs to be adjusted. My intention is to engage students in considering evaluative criteria. Two, I ask students to be engaged in modifying the rubric because I want students to feel ownership for the criteria. I want them to have a say in how their writing will be evaluated. Three, I ask students to join with me in evaluating the rubric because I get lots of goodwill points. Students are quite amazed that a professor would actually let them help make decisions about how their papers are graded. It appears that my invitation to them to be actively involved in making decisions about grading criteria is unheard of. But students like to be included. They like to be treated as adults who are capable of adding value to the class and have the authority to make decisions directly affecting their grade.

> [Students] like to be treated as adults who are capable of adding value to the class and have the authority to make decisions directly affecting their grade.

The rubric in Figure 7 combines two evaluative concepts. One, criteria and point values are transparent. Two, evaluation is a matter of corporate decision making. Writers, peers, and professor have a say in the final grade, as the columns marked Self, Peer, and Teacher suggest. The weight given to each participant in summative evaluation can vary. For instance, "self" can be worth 25 percent of the final grade, "peer" another 25 percent, and "teacher" 50 percent. Or the professor can make self and peer grades advisory only. The chief value of a rubric is its power to make summative evaluative criteria transparent. Whether professors add to that transparency the authority for writers and peers to participate in summative evaluation is a matter for each professor to determine. Because the rubric represents criteria that will be used during formative evaluation so that students can meet the expectations of summative evaluation, professors need to engage students in using the rubric throughout the writing process. For instance, professors can ask students to complete copies of the rubric during peer evaluation.

Methods of Assigning Grades

Although a rubric can be considered a method of assigning grades, I have separated rubrics from the question of how to address the issue of group and individual grades. Thus, this section focuses on three methods professors can use to determine the relationship between group and individual effort in collaborative writing projects. I preface these three methods with comments about ways groups can divide the writing task among themselves, because the way a group (or professor) determines who writes what has an impact on methods of summative evaluation.

Groups can divide the writing in three ways: (1) one person does the bulk of the writing, but the other group members provide drafts of sections, references, and comments about the draft the one person is creating; (2) each person in the group writes a section of the paper and then one or more persons in the group edit the combined sections to give the paper consistency; (3) the entire group writes as a group, with half the group members writing together during the early stages of the writing process and, at a certain point, the other half taking over and completing the writing task. The way groups are made up affects how easily individual writing tasks can be separated from the group effort and, in turn, how easily individual efforts can be specified during summative evaluation. Professors can use the following methods during summative evaluation:

Professors can divide grades in parts. One grade is for the final project, the other for the individual's part in the final project. Beard, Rymer, and Williams (1989) divide a student's grade into three parts. Fifty percent of the grade is allotted to the group report, 25 percent to the student's oral interaction with other group members, and the last 25 percent to the student's individual section of the final document. In addition, professors could include data from students' peer evaluations and self-evaluations to determine the final grade. Bosley (1990) also divides the final grade into two parts: a group grade based on the final project and an individual grade based on the student's participation in the group. Bosley refers to task sheets students maintain during the collaborative process to gain insight into their participation in the group. Morgan, Allen, and Atkinson (1989) use a similar method.

Professors can cograde with students. Siders (1983), for instance, provides grading sheets that show how he uses teacher, student, and peer input to determine final grades. Evidence in the literature suggests that students, when trained, can grade as well as professors (Marcoulides and Simkin, 1991, 1995). Ney (1980) also endorses student-graded papers but includes grades for the quality of students' peer grading responses.

Professors can give group grades for group projects and individual grades for individual projects. Under this method, professors give all students in the group one grade based on the quality of the final project. Professors may adjust the grade down for students who have not done their share of the work as evidenced by peer evaluations. Professors also include individual writing assignments. Three reasons can be advanced for this method. First, not all students do their best work in a collaborative writing group, and such students should be given opportunities to do their best work. Professors in disciplines that give privilege of place to the single-author monograph or journal article are probably sympathetic to students who prefer to write individual papers. Second, a student's grade for a course should reflect the student's ability to function in a variety of roles. One of those roles can be membership in a collaborative writing group, but such membership should not preclude other roles, such as individual effort as demonstrated in a single-author writing assignment. Third, a purpose of education is to prepare citizens to interact successfully in the larger social order—indeed, the world social order—and collaborative writing assignments can promote that purpose. But another purpose of education is to encourage individual creativity and inquisitiveness that can be satisfied by following one's own star. Neither purpose should override the other.

Professors can give group members the exclusive right to supply final grades for projects. Barbour (1990) uses a method in which each member of a group grades the other members.

Professors can delay the grade. When grading a group's written project, I collect the final projects and mark them. Then I return the ungraded projects to the groups. Students were expecting grades, so they are surprised, but I tell them that I did not have a chance to look at their best work and give them advice about revision until I reviewed their presentation copies. I note that the groups may not want to or have time to revise. Because I had not informed them of my intentions, a group may not have time to continue working on the project. If a group decides not to revise, group members can return their project to me and I will grade it. I cannot remember a time when a group did not take time to revise the marked paper I returned to the group members. Generally, students express appreciation for the opportunity to revise what they thought was their final draft because I pointed out problems and made suggestions that escaped their peers. Philosophically, I delay giving a final grade because I want students to act upon my comments, and if I connect those comments to a grade, there is no incentive to revise, unless, of course, I would consider giving better grades for revision efforts. But I do not want to do that. I am not interested in having students revise for incremental increases in their grades. I want them to revise with the primary intention of improving their writing and the secondary intention of improving their grade.

Conclusion

This chapter is limited to specific issues related to grading collaborative writing; however, much more can be said about grading student writing, and I invite professors who are interested in a fuller view of how to grade students' writing to consult Speck (2000).

Conclusion and Recommendations

COLLABORATIVE WRITING is one method for promoting active learning; however, I agree with Tomlinson's (1990) comment that writing is basic to learning because writing "is perhaps the best single activity to generate and organize thought" (p. 38). I suggest, therefore, that writing is indispensable in the classroom that seeks to help students learn actively. At the same time, I agree with Tomlinson's comment that "the use of writing as a way to learn is not necessarily quick and simple. Requiring daily or frequent writing is not an easier way to teach" (p. 34). As a professor of English who has academic credentials in rhetoric and composition and who has taught writing extensively in the academy, I can attest to the fact that teaching writing is no work for those who want quick and simple methods of helping students to learn actively. For professors to use writing effectively in their classes, they need not only to know why writing is important (theoretical considerations) but also to integrate writing into their teaching (pedagogical considerations)—and theory and pedagogy are interrelated. For professors to enthusiastically endorse the use of writing in their classrooms without a due regard for the theoretical issues that undergird the pedagogical use of writing is to court disappointment and potential disaster. My hope is that this monograph will supply a theoretical foundation for the use of collaborative writing in college and university classrooms. In addition, I have provided various pedagogical practices that may be useful in and of themselves but, more important, give professors models that they can adapt to their own particular classrooms. Based on the information in this monograph, I make the following recommendations:

Professors should become students of the writing process. I have made the bold claim that all professors should teach writing, and in making that claim, I have noted that professors across the disciplines need to know how to teach writing. The two claims seem to me inextricably connected. It is not enough for professors to "use" writing in their classrooms, whatever that means; rather, professors must understand the rudiments of the processes people employ when they write and must articulate those processes to students. Frankly, if professors are themselves writing professionally and if they are evaluating their own writing processes, they will have important insights into writing when they explain to students how to use the writing process. If professors are not writing professionally, they should consider the need to write so that they can speak with authority about the writing process and provide students with examples of their writing to prove that the writing process is messy (recursive) *and* effective.

Professors should rethink their sole reliance on the lecture method as the best medium for promoting active learning. Perhaps the most critical decision professors will make when considering the use of collaborative writing in their classrooms is how to integrate active learning and the lecture method. (I have not advocated, and I do not advocate, the overthrow of the lecture method, so the real issue for me is not the abolition of lectures but the transformation of lectures so that they can promote active learning.) The evidence I have cited about the limits of lectures in promoting active learning—indeed, in promoting learning at all—provides a powerful incentive for professors to critically reevaluate the ways they use lectures. The literature on the lecture method provides an array of collaborative writing methods that can enhance the lecture and help students learn the material professors include in their lectures. Does it not make good theoretical and pedagogical sense to ensure that students have proven opportunities to learn what professors want them to learn?

Professors should consider the need to reevaluate their role in the classroom. Collaborative writing calls into question the traditional role of the professor as the central authority in the classroom. I have affirmed throughout this monograph the necessity of the professor's authority in the classroom, but at the same time I have questioned the traditional ways professors use their authority. Collaborative writing, as a premier method of active learning, requires professors to view students as collaborators and the classroom as a site for active learning, a place where students have the opportunity to be taught by all the other collaborators in the classroom and to teach all the collaborators. I have cited literature on effective teaching that promotes the ideal of such collaboration, and I have stressed the importance of professors' seeing themselves as expert mentors. My own experience in helping students to write collaboratively coupled with the literature on collaborative learning, active learning, and collaborative writing, however, suggests that professors will be better educators when they

> **Collaborative writing, as a premier method of active learning, requires professors to view students as collaborators and the classroom as a site for active learning.**

reconceptualize their role in the classroom so that it includes mentoring and collaborative learning, including collaborative writing. This redefinition of the professor's role includes a reconceptualization of the relationship between formative and summative evaluation so that students are actively engaged in the evaluation process, from beginning to end.

Professors should consider starting with brief collaborative writing assignments and increasing the complexity of the assignments over time. The full-blown collaborative writing assignment is a major commitment of time and resources, so professors will want to start with modest attempts to integrate collaborative writing in their courses and increase the amount of collaborative writing over time. As Paulson (1999) notes, "The process of changing my classroom from one of lecture to one where active learning and group learning are used was gradual. It is a mistake to go from lecture to active learning overnight. It takes a fair amount of practice and experimentation to learn how to effectively employ active learning in the classroom" (p. 1139). Begin with a minute paper in one class. Evaluate the results of introducing the minute paper. Try other short collaborative writing assignments and begin to see how to integrate collaborative learning into the classroom to promote active learning.

Professors should plan, plan, plan—for potential problems. Collaborative writing assignments, particularly the full-blown assignment I have highlighted in this monograph, have great potential for problems of all kinds. Professors should not begin a full-blown collaborative writing assignment without carefully planning the assignment, from beginning to end. I have provided detailed information about planning and cited numerous sources that can give even more information about planning for both professors and students. I recommend that professors ground themselves in that literature before beginning a full-fledged collaborative writing project. Because collaborative writing assignments take place in a dynamic situation with particular students, who have particular viewpoints, needs, ambitions, and misconceptions, the potential for a collaborative writing assignment to go awry is very real, and professors must manage the collaborative writing process, from beginning to end.

Professors should continue to investigate the claims and methods of those who endorse collaborative writing. The literature on collaborative writing is extensive (Speck, Johnson, Dice, and Heaton, 1999), so professors have a great deal of evidence to support collaborative writing in higher education classrooms and to provide warnings and pointers about the use of collaborative writing in those classrooms. In addition, the literature on collaborative learning and active learning is substantial in volume, theory, and practice. More is being produced as I write. One of our responsibilities as professors is to increase our understanding about classroom pedagogy. Professors by and large have not been accustomed to including literature about classroom teaching in their professional reading, which is unfortunate, because teaching is central to the professorial role. The references I have cited provide a good starting point for diving into the literature on active learning, collaborative learning, and collaborative writing. Reading about classroom pedagogy can keep professors informed about current theory in teaching and learning and can lead to new and vital classroom experiences.

References

Allaei, S. K., and Connor, U. M. (1990). Exploring the dynamics of cross-cultural collaboration in writing classrooms. *Writing Instructor, 10*(1), 19–28.

Angelo, T. A., and Cross, K. P. (1993). *Classroom assessment techniques: A handbook for college teachers* (2nd ed.). San Francisco: Jossey-Bass.

Anson, C., Brady, L., and Larson, M. (1993). Collaboration in practice. *Writing on the Edge, 4*(2), 80–96.

Arbur, R. (1977). The student-teacher conference. *College Composition and Communication, 28*(4), 338–342.

Arms, V. M. (1983). Collaborative writing on a word processor. In *Conference record: The many facets of computer communications* (pp. 85–86). New York: Institute of Electrical and Electronic Engineers Professional Communication Society.

Arms, V. M. (1985). The computer: An aid to collaborative writing. *Technical Writing Teacher, 11*(3), 181–185.

Atwood, J. W. (1992). Collaborative writing: The "other" game in town. *Writing Instructor, 12*(1), 13–26.

Aughterson, K. (2000). Redefining the plain style: Francis Bacon, linguistic extension, and the semantic change in the advancement of learning. *Studies in Philology, 97*(1), 96–143.

Autrey, K. (1987). *The personal journal in composition instruction: A history.* Paper presented at the annual meeting of the Conference on College Composition and Communication, Atlanta, GA. (ED 282 250)

Bailey, G. D., and Dyck, N. (1990). The administrator and cooperative learning: Roles and responsibilities in instructional leadership. *Clearing House, 64*(1), 39–43.

Baiocco, S. A., and DeWaters, J. N. (1998). Successful college teaching: Problem-solving strategies of distinguished professors. Old Tappan, NJ: Allyn & Bacon.

Baker, M. A. (1986). Implementing the company approach in business communication classes. *Bulletin of the Association for Business Communication, 49,* 23–25.

Barbour, D. H. (1990). Collaborative writing in the business writing classroom: An ethical dilemma for the teacher. *Bulletin of the Association for Business Communication, 53*(3), 33–35.

Batson, T. (1988, February). The ENFI project: A networked classroom approach to writing instruction. *Academic Computing,* 32–33, 55–56.

Bean, J. C. (1996). *Engaging ideas: The professor's guide to integrating writing, critical thinking, and active learning in the classroom.* San Francisco: Jossey-Bass.

Beard, J. D., Rymer, J., and Williams, D. L. (1989). An assessment system for collaborative-writing groups: Theory and empirical evaluation. *Journal of Business and Technical Communication, 3*(2), 29–51.

Beason, L. (1993). Feedback and revision in writing across the curriculum classes. *Research in the Teaching of English, 27*(4), 395–422.

Belanger, K., and Greer, J. (1992). Beyond the group project: A blueprint for a collaborative writing course. *Journal of Business and Technical Communication, 6*(1), 99–115.

Belenky, M., Clinchy, B., Goldberger, N., and Tarule, J. (1986). *Women's ways of knowing: The development of self, voice, and mind.* New York: Basic Books.

Bendixen, A. (1986, April 27). It was a mess: How Henry James and others actually wrote a novel. *New York Times Book Review,* 3, 28–29.

Benesch, S. (1984). *Improving peer response: Collaboration between teachers and students.* Paper presented at the annual meeting of the Conference on College Composition and Communication, New York, NY. (ED 243 113)

Bernhardt, S. A., and Appleby, B. C. (1985). Collaboration in professional writing with the computer: Results of a survey. *Computers and Composition, 3*(1), 29–42.

Biggs, J. (1996). Enhancing teaching through constructive alignment. *Higher Education, 32,* 347–364.

Bishop, W. (1995). Co-authoring changes the writing classroom: Students authorizing the self, authoring together. *Freshman English News, 23*(1), 54–62.

Bissland, J. H. (1980). Peer evaluation model promotes sharper writing. *Journalism Educator, 34*(4), 17–19.

Bonetti, K. (1988). An interview with Louise Erdrich and Michael Dorris. *Missouri Review, 11*(2), 79–99.

Bonwell, C. C., and Eison, J. A. (1991). *Active learning: Creating excitement in the classroom.* ASHE-ERIC Higher Education Report (vol. 20, no. 1). Washington, DC: School of Education and Human Development, The George Washington University.

Bosley, D. S. (1990). Individual evaluations in a collaborative report project. *Technical Communication, 37,* 160–162.

Bosley, D. S. (1993). Cross-cultural collaboration: Whose culture is it, anyway? *Technical Communication Quarterly, 2*(1), 51–62.

Bosley, D. S., and Jacobs, J. (1992). Collaborative writing: A philosopher's guide. *Teaching Philosophy, 15*(1), 17–32.

Bouton, K., and Tutty, G. (1975, Fall). The effect of peer-evaluated student compositions on writing improvement. *The English Record, 26,* 64–67.

Bowen, B. A. (1993). Using conferences to support the writing process. In A. M. Penrose and B. M. Sitko (Eds.), *Hearing ourselves think: Cognitive research in the college writing classroom* (pp. 188–200). New York: Oxford University Press.

Brady, L. (1994). Collaboration as conversation: Literary cases. In J. S. Leonard, C. S. Wharton, R. M. Davis, and J. Harris (Eds.), *Authority and textuality: Current views of collaborative writing,* no. 14, Locust Hill Literary Studies (pp. 149–168). West Cornwall, CT: Locust Hill Press.

Brooker, J. S. (1994). Common ground and collaboration in T. S. Eliot. In J. S. Leonard, C. S. Wharton, R. M. Davis, and J. Harris (Eds.), *Authority and textuality: Current views of collaborative writing,* no. 14, Locust Hill Literary Studies (pp. 61–74). West Cornwall, CT: Locust Hill Press.

Brown, J. L. (1984, February). Helping students help themselves: Peer evaluation of writing. *Curriculum Review, 23,* 47–50.

Brown, R. E. (1985, Spring). The Dryden-Lee collaboration: *Oedipus* and *The Duke of Guise. Restoration, 9,* 12–25.

Brown-Guillory, E. (1987). The wheel of fortune: Peer grouping and collaborative writing. *Exercise Exchange, 33*(1), 17–18.

Brozick, J. R. (1992). Profiles in collaborative planning: An inquiry into the attitudes of two student writers. In L. Norris and others (Eds.), *Discoveries and dialogues: The making thinking visible casebook* (pp. 42–51). Pittsburgh: Center for the Study of Writing. (ED 348 670)

Bruffee, K. A. (1987). The art of collaborative learning. *Change, 19*(2), 42–47.

Brumback, T. B., Jr. (1985). Peer response: An effective way to incorporate writing into the classroom. *NACTA Journal, 29*(1), 77–81.

Buechler, S. (1983). *Does seeing what I say help me know what I think? Four students revising.* Paper presented at the annual meeting of the Conference on College Composition and Communication, Detroit, MI. (ED 230 941)

Burnett, R. E. (1990). Benefits of collaborative planning in the business communication classroom. *Bulletin of the Association for Business Communication, 53*(2), 9–17.

Burnett, R. E. (1991). Substantive conflict in cooperative context: A way to improve the collaborative planning of workplace documents. *Technical Communication, 38*(4), 532–539.

Burnett, R. E. (1993). Conflict in collaborative decision-making. In N. R. Blyler and C. Thralls (Eds.), *Professional communication: The social perspective* (pp. 144–162). Newbury Park, CA: Sage.

Burnett, R. E. (1994). Decision-making during the collaborative planning of coauthors. In A. M. Penrose and B. M. Sikto (Eds.), *Hearing Ourselves Think: Cognitive research in the college writing classroom. Social and cognitive studies in writing and literacy* (pp. 125–146). New York: Oxford University Press.

Burnett, R. E. (1994). Productive and unproductive conflict in collaboration. In L. Flower, D. L. Wallace, L. Norris, and R. E. Burnett (Eds.), *Making thinking visible: Writing, collaborative planning, and classroom inquiry* (pp. 237–242). Urbana, IL: National Council of Teachers of English.

Burnett, R. E., and Ewald, H. R. (1994). Rabbit trails, ephemera, and other stories: Feminist methodology and collaborative research. *Journal of Advanced Composition, 14*(1), 21–51.

Campbell, J. A. (1996). Oratory, democracy, and the classroom. In R. Soder (Ed.), *Democracy, education, and the schools* (pp. 211–243). San Francisco: Jossey-Bass.

Cannon, S. I. (1989). The reading of literature and responding to student writing. *Journal of Teaching Writing, 8,* 239–254.

Carnicelli, T. A. (1980). The writing conference: A one-to-one conversation. In T. R. Donovan and B. W. McClelland (Eds.), *Eight approaches to teaching composition* (pp. 101–131). Urbana, IL: National Council of Teachers of English.

Carson, J. G., and Nelson, G. L. (1994). Writing groups: Cross-cultural issues. *Journal of Second Language Writing, 3*(1), 17–30.

Carton, K. (1990, October). Collaborative writing of mathematics problems. *Mathematics Teacher,* 542–544.

Charney, D. (1994). The effect of hypertext on processes of reading and writing. In C. L. Selfe and S. Hilligoss (Eds.), *Literacy and computers: The complications of teaching and learning with technology* (pp. 238–263). New York: Modern Language Association of America.

Chickering, A. W., and Gamson, Z. F. (1987, March). Seven principles for good practice. *AAHE Bulletin, 39,* 3–7.

Chiseri-Strater, E. (1991). *Academic literacies: The public and private discourse of university students.* Portsmouth, NH: Boynton/Cook.

Collins, V. T. (1989). Personality type and collaborative writing. In R. Louth and A. M. Scott (Eds.), *Collaborative technical writing: Theory and practice* (pp. 111–116). Hammond, LA: Association of Teachers of Technical Writing.

Connors, P. E. (1990). Collaborative learning in the technical writing classroom. In *Proceedings of the 37th international technical communication conference. Communication: In the chips* (pp. ET-3–ET-33). Arlington, VA: Society for Technical Communication.

Connors, R. J. (1985). Mechanical correctness as a focus in composition instruction. *College Composition and Communication, 36*(1), 61–72.

Connors, R. J., and Lunsford, A. A. (1988). Frequency of formal errors in current writing, or Ma and Pa Kettle do research. *College Composition and Communication, 39*(4), 395–409.

Connors, R. J., and Lunsford, A. A. (1993). Teachers' rhetorical comments on student papers. *College Composition and Communication, 44*(2), 200–223.

Cooper, J. L., and Robinson, P. (2000). Getting started: Informal small-group strategies in large classes. In J. MacGregor and others (Eds.), *Strategies for energizing large classes: From small groups to learning communities.* New Directions for Teaching and Learning, no. 81 (pp. 17–24). San Francisco: Jossey-Bass.

Cooper, J. L., Robinson, P., and McKinney, M. (1994). Cooperative learning in the classroom. In D. F. Halpern and Associates (Eds.), *Changing college classrooms: New teaching and learning strategies for an increasingly complex world* (pp. 74–92). San Francisco: Jossey-Bass.

Coppola, N. W. (1996). Computer-mediated conferencing: Teaching in a virtual classroom. In *Proceedings of the 43rd annual conference: Evolution/revolution* (pp. 41–43). Arlington, VA: Society for Technical Communication.

Corder, J. W. (1989). Asking for a text and trying to learn it. In B. Lawson, S. S. Ryan, and W. R. Winterowd (Eds.), *Encountering student texts: Interpretive issues in reading student writing* (pp. 89–97). Urbana, IL: National Council of Teachers of English.

Cornell, C., and Newton, R. (1988). *Collaborative revision on a computer.* Paper presented at the annual meeting of the Conference on College Composition and Communication, St. Louis, MO. (ED 295 155)

Couture, B., and Rymer, J. (1991). Discourse interaction between writer and supervisor: A primary collaboration in workplace writing. In M. M. Lay and W. M. Karis (Eds.), *Collaborative writing in industry: Investigations in theory and practice* (pp. 87–108). Amityville, NY: Baywood.

Cross, G. A. (1990). A Bakhtinian exploration of factors affecting the collaborative writing of an executive letter of an annual report. *Research in the Teaching of English, 24,* 173–203.

Cyganowski, C. K. (1990). The computer classroom and collaborative learning: The impact on student writers. In C. Handa (Ed.), *Computers and community: Teaching composition in the twenty-first century* (pp. 68–88). Portsmouth, NH: Boynton/Cook Heinemann.

Daiker, D. A. (1989). Learning to praise. In C. M. Anson (Ed.), *Writing and response: Theory, practice, and research* (pp. 103–113). Urbana, IL: National Council of Teachers of English.

Dale, H. (1997). *Co-authoring in the classroom: Creating an environment for effective collaboration.* Urbana, IL: National Council of Teachers of English.

Danis, F. (1982). *Weaving the web of meaning: Interaction patterns in peer-response groups.* Paper presented at the annual meeting of the Conference on College Composition and communication, San Francisco, CA. (ED 214 202)

Dansereau, D. F. (1988). Cooperative learning strategies. In C. E. Weinstein, E. T. Goetz, and P. Alexander (Eds.), *Learning and study strategies: Issues in assessment, instruction, and evaluation* (pp. 103–120). San Diego: Academic Press.

Dautermann, J. (1993). Negotiating meaning in a hospital discourse community. In R. Spilka (Ed.), *Writing in the workplace: New research perspectives* (pp. 98–110). Carbondale and Edwardsville: Southern Illinois University Press.

Davis, B. G. (1993). *Tools for teaching.* San Francisco: Jossey-Bass.

Davis, K. (1991). Hypertext as a medium for student collaboration. In E. Hansen (Ed.), *Collaborative learning in higher education. Proceedings of the teaching conference.* Bloomington, IN. (ED 335 984)

Debs, M. B. (1991). Recent research on collaborative writing in industry. *Technical Communication, 38*(4), 476–484.

Dillon, A. (1993). How collaborative is collaborative writing? An analysis of the production of two technical reports. In M. Sharples (Ed.), *Computer supported collaborative writing* (pp. 69–85). London: Springer-Verlag.

Duin, A. H., and Hansen, C. (1994). Reading and writing on computer networks as social construction and social interaction. In C. L. Selfe and S. Hilligoss (Eds.), *Literacy and computers: The complications of teaching and learning with technology* (pp. 89–112). New York: Modern Language Association of America.

Duin, A. H., Jorn, L. A., and DeBower, M. S. (1991). Collaborative writing: Courseware and telecommunications. In M. M. Lay and W. M. Karis (Eds.), *Collaborative writing in industry: Investigations in theory and practice* (pp. 146–169). Amityville, NY: Baywood.

Duke, C. R. (1975). The student-centered conference and the writing process. *English Journal, 64*(9), 44–47.

Ede, L., and Lunsford, A. (1990). *Singular texts/plural authors: Perspectives on collaborative writing.* Carbondale and Edwardsville: Southern Illinois University Press.

Elbow, P. (1981). *Writing with power: Techniques for mastering the writing process.* New York: Oxford University Press.

Elbow, P., and Belanoff, P. (1989). *Sharing and responding.* New York: Random House.

Eldred, J. M. (1989). Computers, composition pedagogy, and the social view. In G. E. Hawisher and S. L. Selfe (Eds.), *Critical perspectives on computers and composition instruction* (pp. 201–218). New York: Teachers College Press.

Elsbree, L. (1985). Learning to write through mutual coaching. In J. Katz (Ed.), *Teaching as though students mattered,* New Directions for Teaching and Learning, no. 21 (pp. 23–29). San Francisco: Jossey-Bass.

Enos, R. L. (1993). Classical rhetoric and group writing: A warranted relationship. In T. Enos (Ed.), *Learning from the histories of rhetoric: Essays in honor of Winifred Bryan Horner* (pp. 144–155). Carbondale and Edwardsville: Southern Illinois University Press.

Epstein, J. (Ed.). (1981). *Masters: Portraits of great teachers.* New York: Basic Books.

Ericksen, S. C. (1984). *The essence of good teaching: Helping students learn and remember what they learn.* San Francisco: Jossey-Bass.

Ewald, H. R., and MacCallum, V. (1990). Promoting creative tension within collaborative writing groups. *Bulletin of the Association for Business Communication, 53*(2), 23–26.

Faigley, L. (1990). Subverting the electronic notebook: Teaching writing using networked computers. In D. A. Daiker and M. Morenberg (Eds.), *The writing teachers as researcher: Essays in the theory and practice of class-based research* (pp. 290–311). Portsmouth, NH: Boynton/Cook.

Fassler, B. (1978). The red pen revisited: Teaching composition through student conferences. *College English, 40*(2), 186–190.

Fedje, Cheryl G., and Essex-Buss, L. (1989). Words of wisdom—theirs not mine: Evaluating students' writing. *Illinois Teacher, 32*(5), 190–193.

Felder, R. M., and Brent, R. (1996). Navigating the bumpy road to student-centered instruction. *College Teaching, 44*(2), 43–47.

Field, L. (1987). *Thomas Wolfe and his editors: Establishing a true text for the posthumous publications.* Norman: University of Oklahoma Press.

Fish, R. S., Kraut, R. E., Leland, M.D.P., and Cohen, M. (1988). Quilt: A collaborative tool for cooperative writing. In R. B. Allen (Ed.), *Proceedings of the conference on office information systems* (pp. 30–37). Baltimore: Association for Computing Machinery.

Flower, L., and Ackerman, J. (1994). *Writers at work: Strategies for communicating in business and professional settings.* New York: Harcourt Brace.

Flower, L., and Hayes, J. R. (1981). A cognitive process theory of writing. *College Composition and Communication, 32,* 365–387.

Flower, L., and Higgins, L. (1991). *Collaboration and the construction of meaning.* Technical Report no. 56. Berkeley, CA: Center for the Study of Writing. (ED 341 069)

Flower, L., Wallace, D. L., Norris, L., and Burnett, R. E. (Eds.). (1994). *Making thinking visible: Writing, collaborative planning, and classroom inquiry.* Urbana, IL: National Council of Teachers of English.

Flynn, E. A. (1982). *Freedom, restraint, and peer group interaction.* Paper presented at the annual meeting of the Conference on College Composition and Communication, San Francisco, CA. (ED 216 365)

Flynn, E. A., and others. (1991). Gender and modes of collaboration in a chemical engineering design course. *Journal of Business and Technical Communication, 5*(4), 444–462.

Folks, J. J. (1979). Improving rough drafts: An evaluation sheet technique. *Journal of Developmental and Remedial Education, 2*(3), 7–8.

Forman, J. (1989). The discourse communities and group writing practices of management students. In C. B. Matalene (Ed.), *Worlds of writing: Teaching and learning in discourse communities of work* (pp. 247–254). New York: Random House.

Forman, J. (1990). Leadership dynamics of computer-supported writing groups. *Computers and Composition, 7*(2), 35–46.

Forman, J. (1994). Literacy, collaboration, and technology: New connections and challenges. In C. L. Selfe and S. Hilligoss (Eds.), *Literacy and computers: The complications of teaching and learning with technology* (pp. 130–143). New York: Modern Language Association of America.

Fosnot, C. T. (1991). *Enquiring teachers, enquiring learners: A constructivist approach for teaching.* New York: Teachers College Press.

Frederick, P. (1986). The lively lecture. *College Teaching, 34*(2), 43–50.

Fulwiler, T. (1986). The argument for writing across the curriculum. In A. Young and T. Fulwiler (Eds.), *Writing across the disciplines: Research into practice* (pp. 21–32). Portsmouth, NH: Heinemann.

Fulwiler, T. (1987). *The journal book.* Upper Montclair, NJ: Boynton/Cook.

Fulwiler, T., Gorman, M. E., and Gorman, M. E. (1986). Changing faculty attitudes toward writing. In A. Young and T. Fulwiler (Eds.), *Writing across the disciplines: Research into practice* (pp. 53–67). Portsmouth, NH: Heinemann.

Galegher, J., and Kraut, R. E. (1990). Computer-mediated communication for intellectual teamwork: A field experiment in group writing. In *Proceedings of the CSCW'90* (pp. 65–78). New York: The Association for Computing Machinery.

Gee, T. C. (1972). Students' responses to teacher comments. *Research in the Teaching of English, 6*(2), 212–221.

George, D. (1984). Working with peer groups in the composition classroom. *College Composition and Communication, 35*(3), 320–326.

Gere, A. R. (1982). Students' oral response to written compositions. (ED 229 781)

Gerlach, J. M. (1994). Is this collaboration? In K. Bosworth and S. Hamilton (Eds.), *Collaborative learning: Underlying processes and effective techniques* (pp. 5–14). New Directions for Teaching and Learning, no. 59. San Francisco: Jossey-Bass.

Gerson, S. M. (1993). Commentary: Teaching technical writing in a collaborative computer classroom. *Journal of Technical Writing and Communication, 23*(1), 23–31.

Geske, J. (1992). Overcoming the drawbacks of the large lecture class. *College Teaching, 40*(4), 151–154.

Goldstein, J. R., and Malone, E. L. (1984). Journals on interpersonal and group communication: Facilitating technical project groups. *Journal of Technical Writing and Communication, 14*(2), 113–131.

Goldstein, J. R., and Malone, E. L. (1985). Using journals to strengthen collaborative writing. *Bulletin of the Association for Business Communication, 48*(3), 24–28.

Greenbaum, S., and Taylor, J. (1981). The recognition of usage errors by instructors of freshman composition. *College Composition and Communication, 32*(2), 169–174.

Griffin, D. (1987). Augustan collaboration. *Essays in Criticism, 37*(1), 1–10.

Grimm, N. (1986). Improving students' responses to their peers' essays. *College Composition and Communication, 37*(1), 91–94.

Guyer, C., and Petry, M. (1991). Notes for "Izme Pass" exposé. *Writing on the Edge, 2*(2), 82–89.

Haas, C., and Neuwirth, C. M. (1994). Writing the technology that writes us: Research on literacy and the shape of technology. In C. L. Selfe and S. Hilligoss (Eds.), *Literacy and computers: The complications of teaching and learning with technology* (pp. 319–335). New York: Modern Language Association of America.

Hacker, D. J., and Niederhauser, D. S. (2000). Promoting deep and durable learning in the online classroom. In R. E. Weiss, D. S. Knowlton, and B. W. Speck (Eds.), *Principles of effective teaching in the online classroom.* New Directions for Teaching and Learning, no. 84 (pp. 53–63). San Francisco: Jossey-Bass.

Halsted, I. (1974). Putting error in its place. *Journal of Basic Writing, 1*(1), 72–86.

Handa, C. (1990). Politics, ideology, and the strange, slow death of the isolated composer, or why we need community in the writing classroom. In C. Handa (Ed.), *Computers and community: Teaching composition in the twenty-first century* (pp. 160–184). Portsmouth, NH: Boynton/Cook.

Harris, J. (1997). *A teaching subject: Composition since 1966.* Upper Saddle River, NJ: Prentice Hall.

Harris, M. (1978). Evaluation: The process for revision. *Journal of Basic Writing, 1*(4), 82–90.

Harris, M. (1986). *Teaching one-to-one: The writing conference.* Urbana, IL: National Council of Teachers of English.

Harris, M. (1990). Teacher/student talk: The collaborative conference. In S. Hynds and D. L. Rubin (Eds.), *Perspectives on talk and learning* (pp. 149–162). Urbana, IL: National Council of Teachers of English.

Harris, M. (1992). Collaboration is not collaboration is not collaboration: Writing center tutorials vs. peer-response groups. *College Composition and Communication, 43*(3), 369–383.

Hartley, J. (1984). The role of colleagues and text-editing programs in improving texts. *IEEE Transactions on Professional Communication, PC-27*(1), 42–44.

Hawisher, G. E. (1992). Electronic meetings of the minds: Research, electronic conferences, and composition studies. In G. E. Hawisher and P. LeBlanc (Eds.), *Re-imagining computers and composition: Teaching and research in the virtual age* (pp. 81–101). Portsmouth, NH: Boynton/Cook Heinemann.

Hawisher, G. E., and Selfe, C. L. (1991). The rhetoric of technology and the electronic writing class. *College Composition and Communication, 42*(1), 55–65.

Hawisher, G. E., and Selfe, C. L. (1999). The passions that mark us: Teaching, texts, and technologies. In G. E. Hawisher and C. L. Selfe (Eds.), *Passions, pedagogies, and 21st century technologies* (pp. 1–12). Logan: Utah State University Press.

Haws, R., and Engel, R. (1987). When one plus one equals one: Hadley Irwin. *Children's Literature in Education, 18*(4), 195–201.

Hayes, M. F., and Daiker, D. A. (1984). Using protocol analysis in evaluating responses to student writing. *Freshman English News, 13*(2), 1–4, 10.

Hays, J. (1982). Facilitating the peer critiquing of writing. In C. Carter (Ed.), *Structuring for success in the English classroom: Classroom practices in teaching English, 1981–1982* (pp. 113–119). Urbana, IL: National Council of Teachers of English.

Healy, M. K. (1983). Using student writing response groups in the classroom. In G. Camp (Ed.), *Teaching writing: Essays from the Bay Area Writing Project* (pp. 266–267). Portsmouth, NH: Boynton/Cook.

Heffernan, J.A.W. (1983). *Getting the red out: Grading without degrading.* Paper presented at the annual meeting of the Conference on College Composition and Communication, Detroit, MI. (ED 229 788)

Henson, L., and Sutliff, K. (1998). A service learning approach to business and technical writing instruction. *Journal of Technical Writing and Communication, 28*(2), 189–205.

Higgins, L., Flower, L., and Petraglia, J. (1990). *Planning text together: The role of critical reflection in student collaboration.* Paper presented at the annual meeting of the American Educational Research Association, Boston, MA. (ED 322 495)

Hirsch, E. D., and Harrington, D. P. (1981). Measuring the communicative effectiveness of prose. In C. H. Frederieksen and J. F. Dominic (Eds.), *Writing: The nature, development, and teaching of written communication* (Vol. 2, pp. 189–207). Hillsdale, NJ: Erlbaum.

Holt, M. (1992). The value of written peer criticism. *College Composition and Communication, 43*(3), 384–392.

Hopson, E. H. (1998). Designing and grading writing assignments. In R. S. Anderson and B. W. Speck (Eds.), *Changing the way we grade student performance: Classroom assessment and the new learning paradigm.* New Directions in Teaching and Learning, no. 74 (pp. 51–57). San Francisco: Jossey-Bass.

Huber, R. M. (1992). *How professors play the cat guarding the cream.* Fairfax, VA: George Mason University Press.

Hulbert, J. E. (1994). Developing collaborative insights and skills. *Bulletin of the Association for Business Communication, 57*(2), 53–56.

Hutchings, P. (1996). *Making teaching community property: A menu for peer collaboration and peer review.* Washington, DC: American Association for Higher Education.

Inge, M. T. (1994). Mark Twain and Dan Beard's collaborative *Connecticut Yankee.* In J. S. Leonard, C. S. Wharton, R. M. Davis, and J. Harris (Eds.), *Authority and textuality: Current views of collaborative writing,* no. 14, Locust Hill Literary Studies (pp. 169–227). West Cornwall, CT: Locust Hill Press.

Irby, J. R. (1995). Editorial conference dialogues in the news laboratory. *Journalism Educator, 50*(1), 63–78.

Issler, K. (1983). A conception of excellence in teaching. *Education, 103,* 338–343.

Jehn, K. A. (1997). A qualitative analysis of conflict types and dimensions in organizational groups. *Administrative Science Quarterly, 42,* 530–557.

Jensen, G. H., and DiTiberio, J. K. (1984). Personality and individual writing processes. *College Composition and Communication, 35*(3), 285–300.

Jipson, J., and Paley, N. (2000). Because no one gets there alone: Collaboration as co-mentoring. *Theory into Practice, 39*(1), 36–42.

Johnson, D. W., and Johnson, R. T. (1979). Conflict in the classroom: Controversy and learning. *Review of Educational Research, 49*(1), 51–69.

Johnson, D. W., and Johnson, R. T. (1986). Computer-assisted cooperative learning. *Educational Technology, 26,* 12–18.

Johnson, D. W., Johnson, R. T., and Smith, K. A. (1991). *Cooperative learning: Increasing college faculty instructional productivity.* ASHE-ERIC Higher Education Report (vol. 20, no. 4). Washington, DC: Graduate School of Education and Human Development, The George Washington University.

Johnson, D. W., Johnson, R. T., and Smith, K. A. (1998). Cooperative learning returns to college: What evidence is there that it works? *Change, 30*(4), 27–35.

Karis, B. (1989). Conflict in collaboration: A Burkean perspective. *Rhetoric Review, 8*(1), 113–126.

Kaye, A. R. (1993). Computer networking for development of distance education courses. In M. Sharples (Ed.), *Computer supported collaborative writing* (pp. 41–67). London: Springer-Verlag.

Kearsley, G. (1988). Authoring considerations for hypertext. *Educational Technology, 28*(11), 21–24.

Kemp, F. (1993). Student to students: Putting computers in writing classrooms. In L. Myers (Ed.), *Approaches to computer writing classrooms* (pp. 19–34). Albany: State University of New York Press.

Kiesler, S., Siegel, J., and McGuire, T. W. (1984). Social psychological aspects of computer-mediated communication. *American Psychologist, 39,* 1123–1134.

Kinkead, J. (1988, November). Wired: Computer networks in the English classroom. *English Journal,* 39–41.

Knodt, E. A. (1994). What do you think? Collaborative learning and critical thinking in the business writing class. In J. S. Leonard, C. E. Wharton, R. M. Davis, and J. Harris (Eds.), *Authority and textuality: Current views of collaborative writing*, no. 14, Locust Hill Literary Studies (pp. 113–123). West Cornwall, CT: Locust Hill Press.

Knox-Quinn, C. (1990). Collaboration in the writing classroom: An interview with Ken Kesey. *College Composition and Communication, 41*(3), 309–317.

Kowalski, R. (1989, April). Computer conferencing in the English composition classroom. *Educational Technology, 29*–32.

Lamberg, W. (1977, May). Feedback on writing: Much more than teacher correction. *Statement: The Journal of the Colorado Language Arts Society, 12,* 33–38.

Lamberg, W. (1980). Self-provided and peer-provided feedback. *College Composition and Communication, 31*(1), 63–69.

Langston, M. D., and Batson, T. W. (1990). The social shifts invited by working collaboratively on computer networks: The ENFI project. In C. Handa (Ed.), *Computers and community: Teaching composition in the twenty-first century* (pp. 140–159). Portsmouth, NH: Boynton/Cook.

Laumer, K. (1977). How to collaborate without getting your head shaved. In D. Knight (Ed.), *Turning points: Essays on the art of science fiction* (pp. 215–217). New York: Harper.

Lawson, B., and Ryan, S. S. (1989). Introduction: Interpretive issues in student writing. In B. Lawson, S. S. Ryan, and W. R. Winterowd (Eds.), *Encountering student texts: Interpretive issues in reading student writing* (pp. vii–xvii). Urbana, IL: National Council of Teachers of English.

Lay, M. M. (1982). Procedures, instructions, and specifications: A challenge in audience analysis. *Journal of Technical Writing and Communication, 12*(3), 235–242.

Lay, M. M. (1989). Interpersonal conflict in collaborative writing: What we can learn from gender studies. *Journal of Business and Technical Communication, 3*(2), 5–28.

Lay, M. M. (1992). The androgynous collaborator: The impact of gender studies on collaboration. In J. Forman (Ed.), *New visions of collaborative writing* (pp. 82–104). Portsmouth, NH: Boynton/Cook.

LeBlanc, P. (1988). How to get the words just right: A reappraisal of word process and revision. *Computers and Composition, 5*(3), 29–42.

Lees, E. O. (1989). The exceptable way of the society: Stanley Fish's theory of reading and the task of the teacher of editing. In P. Donahue and E. Quandahl (Eds.), *Reclaiming pedagogy: The rhetoric of the classroom* (pp. 144–163). Carbondale and Edwardsville: Southern Illinois University Press.

Leverenz, C. S. (1994). Peer response in the multicultural composition classroom: Dissensus—a dream (deferred). *Journal of Advanced Composition, 14*(1), 167–186.

Lewis, B. (1993). Uses of language in collaborative design teams. In *Proceedings of the international professional communication conference. The new face of technical communication: People, processes, products* (pp. 5–10). New York: Institute of Electrical and Electronic Engineers Professional Communication Society.

Locker, K. O. (1992). What makes a collaborative writing team successful? A case study of lawyers and social workers in a state agency. In J. Forman (Ed.), *New Visions of Collaborative Writing* (pp. 37–62). Portsmouth, NH: Boynton/Cook.

MacGregor, J. (1990). Collaborative learning: Shared inquiry as a process of reform. In M. D. Svinicki (Ed.), *The changing face of college teaching* (pp. 19–30). New Directions for Teaching and Learning, no. 42. San Francisco: Jossey-Bass.

MacGregor, J., Cooper, J. L., Smith, K. A., and Robinson, P. (Eds.). (2000). *Strategies for energizing large classes: From small groups to learning communities.* New Directions for Teaching and Learning, no. 73. San Francisco: Jossey-Bass.

MacNealy, M. S., Speck, B. W., and Simpson, B. (1996). Fiddling around with text: Implication for composition from a study of a "non-reviser." *Issues in Writing, 8*(1), 27–53.

Marcoulides, G. A., and Simkin, M. G. (1991, November/December). Evaluating student papers: The case for peer review. *Journal of Education for Business,* 80–83.

Marcoulides, G. A., and Simkin, M. G. (1995). The consistency of peer review in student writing projects. *Journal of Education for Business, 70*(4), 220–223.

Markel, M. (1998). *Technical communication: Situations and strategies* (5th ed.). New York: St. Martin's Press.

Matthews, R. S. (1996). Collaborative learning: Creating knowledge with students. In R. J. Menges, M. Weimer, and Associates (Eds.), *Teaching on solid ground: Using scholarship to improve practice* (pp. 101–124). San Francisco: Jossey-Bass.

McKeachie, W. J. (1999). *Teaching tips: Strategies, research, and theory for college and university teachers* (10th ed.). Boston: Houghton Mifflin.

McLeod, S., and Maimon, E. (2000). Clearing the air: WAC myths and realities. *College English, 62*(5), 573–583.

Mead, D. G. (1994). *Celebrating dissensus in collaboration: A professional writing perspective.* Paper presented at the Conference on College Composition and Communication, Nashville, TN. (ED 375 427)

Merrier, P. A. (1988). Emphasizing teamwork in business writing. *Business Education Forum, 42*(7), 16–25.

Messelaar, D. (1976, Winter). The use of peer rating scales in teaching writing. *The English Record, 27,* 17–19.

Meyers, G. D. (1985). Adapting Zoellner's talk-write to the business writing classroom. *Bulletin of the Association for Business Communication, 48,* 14–16.

Meyers, G. D. (1986). The writing seminar: Broadening peer collaboration in freshman English. *The Writing Instructor, 6*(1), 48–56.

Meyers, G. D. (1988). Using criterion-based and reader-based peer-review sheets. *Bulletin of the Association for Business Communication, 51,* 35–39.

Meyers, G. D. (1989). Write, respond, revise: Using the seminar method to teach technical writing. In R. Louth and A. M. Scott (Eds.), *Collaborative technical writing: Theory and practice* (pp. 129–144). Hammond, LA: Association of Teachers of Technical Writing.

Miller, S. (1984). The student's reader is always a fiction. *Journal of Advanced Composition, 5,* 15–29.

Min, Z., and Rada, R. (1994). MUCH electronic publishing environment: Principles and practices. *Journal of the American Society for Information Science, 45*(5), 300–309.

Morgan, M., Allen, N., and Atkinson, D. (1989). Evaluating collaborative assignments. In R. Louth and A. M. Scott (Eds.), *Collaborative technical writing: Theory and practice* (pp. 83–93). Hammond, LA: Association of Teachers of Technical Writing.

Morris, K. K., and Mead, D. G. (1995). Collaboration, consensus, and "dissoi logoi." *Writing on the Edge, 7*(1), 83–92.

Murray, D. M. (1991). *The craft of revision.* Forth Worth: Holt, Rinehart, and Winston.

Murray, D. M. (1997). Teach writing as a process not product. In V. Villanueva, Jr. (Ed.), *Cross-talk in Comp Theory: A reader* (pp. 3–6). Urbana, IL: National Council of Teachers of English.

Nelson, S. J., and Smith, D. C. (1990). Maximizing cohesion and minimizing conflict in collaborative writing groups. *Bulletin of the Association for Business Communication, 53*(2), 59–62.

Neubert, G. A., and McNelis, S. J. (1990). Peer response: Teaching specific revision suggestions. *English Journal, 79*(5), 52–56.

Neuwirth, C. M., and Wojahn, P. G. (1996). Learning to write: Computer support for a cooperative process. In T. Koschmann (Ed.), *CSCL: Theory and practice of an emerging paradigm* (pp. 147–170). Mahway, NJ: Erlbaum.

Newkirk, T. (1984a). Direction and misdirection in peer response. *College Composition and Communication, 35*(3), 301–311.

Newkirk, T. (1984b). How students read student papers: An exploratory study. *Written Communication, 1*(3), 305–382.

Newman, J. M. (1986). Conferencing: Writing as a collaborative activity. *Educational Perspectives, 24*(1), 11–15.

Newman, R., and Newman, J. (1993). Social writing: Premises and practices in computerized contexts. In M. Sharples (Ed.), *Computer supported collaborative writing* (pp. 29–40). London: Springer-Verlag.

Ney, J. (1980). Student attitudes toward a writing class. *Arizona English Bulletin, 22,* 105–112.

Nystrand, M. (1986). Learning to write by talking about writing: A summary of research on intensive peer review in expository writing instruction at the University of Wisconsin–Madison. In M. Nystrand (Ed.), *The structure of written communication* (pp. 179–211). Orlando, FL: Academic Press.

Nystrand, M., and Brandt, D. (1989). Response to writing as a context for learning to write: Theory, practice, and research. In C. M. Anson (Ed.), *Writing and response: Theory, practice, and research* (pp. 209–230). Urbana, IL: National Council of Teachers of English.

Odell, L., and Goswami, D. (Eds.). (1985). *Writing in nonacademic settings.* New York: Guilford.

O'Donnell, A., and Dansereau, D. F. (1992). Scripted cooperation in student dyads: A method for analyzing and enhancing academic learning and performance. In

R. Hertz-Lazarowitz and N. Miller (Eds.), *Instruction in cooperative groups: The theoretical anatomy of group learning* (pp. 120–141). New York: Cambridge University Press.

O'Donnell, A., and Dansereau, D. F. (1994). Learning from lectures: Effects of cooperative review. *Journal of Experimental Education, 61*(2), 116–125.

Paulson, D. R. (1999). Active learning and cooperative learning in the organic chemistry lecture class. *Journal of Chemical Education, 76*(8), 1136–1140.

Pennisi, L. T., and Lawler, P. (1994). Without a net: Collaborative writing. In W. Bishop and H. Ostrom (Eds.), *Colors of a different horse: Rethinking creative writing theory and pedagogy* (pp. 225–233). Urbana, IL: National Council of Teachers of English.

Perkins, D. (1999). The many faces of constructivism. *Educational Leadership, 57*(3), 6–11.

Pianko, S., and Radzik, A. (1980). The student editing method. *Theory into Practice, 19*(3), 220–224.

Pitts, B. J. (1988). Peer evaluation is effective in writing course. *The Journalism Educator, 43*(2), 84–88.

Plowman, L. (1993). Tracing the evolution of a co-authored text. *Language and Communication, 13*(3), 149–161.

Pomerenke, P. J. (1992). Writers at work: Seventeen writers at a major insurance corporation. *Journal of Business and Technical Communication, 6*(2), 172–186.

Porter, J. E. (1986). Intertextuality and the discourse community. *Rhetoric Review, 5*(1), 34–37.

Purves, A. C. (1984). The teacher as reader: An anatomy. *College English, 46*(3), 259–265.

Rada, R., Michailidis, A., and Wang, W. (1994). Collaborative hypermedia in a classroom setting. *Journal of Educational Multimedia and Hypermedia, 3*(1), 21–36.

Radcliffe, T. (1972). Talk-write composition: A theoretical model proposing the use of speech to improve writing. *Research in the Teaching of English, 6*(2), 187–199.

Raign, K. R., and Sims, B. R. (1993). Gender, persuasion techniques, and collaboration. *Technical Communication Quarterly, 2*(1), 89–104.

Raymond, J. C. (1976). Cross-grading: An experiment in evaluating compositions. *College Composition and Communication, 27*(1), 52–55.

Rehling, L. (1996). Writing together: Gender's effect on collaboration. *Journal of Technical Writing and Communication, 26*(2), 163–176.

Reiff, J. D., and J. E. Middleton. (1983). A model for designing and revising assignments. In P. L. Stock (Ed.), *Forum: Essays on theory and practice in the teaching of writing* (pp. 263–268). Upper Montclair, NJ: Boynton/Cook.

Renshaw, D. B. (1990). In-class collaborative cases. *Bulletin of the Association for Business Communication, 53*(2), 63–65.

Reynolds, R. L. (1988). *Collaboration and community formation in English microcomputer labs.* Paper presented at the 39th annual meeting of the Conference on College Composition and Communication, St. Louis, MO. (ED 299 592)

Roebuck, D. B. (1988). One project with collaborative writing! In B. H. Peeples and G. E. Morse (Eds.), *Proceedings of the southeast regional conference of the association for business communication* (pp. 73–77). (ED 308 565)

Roen, D. H. (1989). Developing effective assignments for second language writers. In D. M. Johnson and D. H. Roen (Eds.), *Richness in writing: Empowering ESL students* (pp. 193–206). New York: Longman.

Rohman, D. G. (1965). Prewriting: The stage of discovery in the writing process. *College Composition and Communication, 16,* 106–112.

Romance, N. R., and Vitale, M. R. (1999). Concept mapping as a tool for learning: Broadening the framework for student-centered instruction. *College Teaching, 47*(2), 74–79.

Rose, A. (1982). Spoken versus written criticism of student writing: Some advantage of the conference method. *College Composition and Communication, 33*(3), 326–331.

Rothstein-Vandergriff, J., and Gilson, J. T. (1988). *Collaboration with basic writers in the composition classroom.* Paper presented at the annual meeting of the Conference on College Composition and Communication, St. Louis, MO. (ED 294 220)

Rushton, J. R., Murray, H. G., and Paunonen, S. V. (1983). Personality, research creativity, and teaching effectiveness in university professors. *Scientometrics, 5*(2), 93–116.

Saroyan, A. (2000). The lecturer: Working with large groups. In J. L. Bess and Associates, *Teaching together, teaching alone: Transforming the structure of teams for teaching* (pp. 87–107). San Francisco: Jossey-Bass.

Sawyer, T. M. (1975). Accountability: Or let others grade your students. *College Composition and Communication, 26*(4), 335–340.

Sawyer, T. M. (1976). External examiners: Separating teaching from grading. *Engineering Education, 66*(4), 344–346.

Scheffler, J. A. (1992). Using collaborative writing groups to teach analysis of an RFP. *Bulletin of the Association for Business Communication, 55*(2), 26–28.

Schiff, P. (1982). Responding to writing: Peer critiques, teacher-student conferences, and essay evaluation. In T. Fulwiler and A. Young (Eds.), *Language connections: Writing and reading across the curriculum* (pp. 153–165). Urbana, IL: National Council of Teachers of English.

Schreiber, E. J. (1996). Workplace teams and writing groups: Team management theory and the collaborative writing process. *Issues in Writing, 8*(1), 54–75.

Schwartz, H. J., and Froehlke, K. (1990). The social context of networked learning: Computers as medium. In E. Hansen (Ed.), *Collaborative learning in higher education. Proceedings of the teaching conference,* Bloomington, IN. (ED 335 984)

Schwegler, R. A. (1991). The politics of reading student papers. In B. Lawson, S. S. Ryan, and W. R. Winterowd (Eds.), *Encountering student texts: Interpretive issues in reading student writing* (pp. 203–225). Urbana, IL: National Council of Teachers of English.

Selfe, C. L. (1987). Creating a computer-supported writing lab: Sharing stories and creating vision. *Computers and Composition, 4*(2), 44–65.

Selfe, C. L. (1992). Computer-based conversations and the changing nature of collaboration. In J. Forman (Ed.), *New visions of collaborative writing* (pp. 147–169). Portsmouth, NH: Boynton/Cook.

Selfe, C. L., and Eilola, J. D. (1988). The tie that binds: Building discourse, communities, and group cohesion through computer-based conferences. *Collegiate Microcomputer, 6*(4), 339–348.

Selfe, C. L., and Wahlstrom, B. J. (1985). An emerging rhetoric of collaboration: Computers, collaboration, and the composing process. (ED 261 384)

Sharp, D. (2000, March 25). Drug industry code proposed on "ghost" writing. *Lancet, 355,* 1084.

Siders, J. A. (1983). Instructor, self and peer review: A formative evaluation triad. *College Student Journal, 17*(2), 141–144.

Sigsbee, D. L., Speck, B. W., and Maylath, B. (Eds.). (1997). *Approaches to teaching non-native English speakers across the curriculum.* New Directions for Teaching and Learning, no. 70. San Francisco: Jossey-Bass.

Sims, G. K. (1989). Student peer review in the classroom: A teaching and grading tool. *Journal of Agronomic Education, 18*(2), 105–108.

Sirc, G. (1991). *One of the things at stake in the peer-group conference: The feminine.* Paper presented at the annual meeting of the Conference on College Composition and Communication, Boston, MA. (ED 332 187)

Skubikowski, K., and Elder, J. (1990). Computers and the social contexts of writing. In C. Handa (Ed.), *Computers and community: Teaching composition in the twenty-first century* (pp. 89–105). Portsmouth, NH: Boynton/Cook Heinemann.

Soder, R. (1996). Teaching the teachers of the people. In R. Soder (Ed.), *Democracy, education, and the schools* (pp. 244–274). San Francisco: Jossey-Bass.

Sommers, N. (1980). Revision strategies of student writers and experienced adult writers. *College Composition and Communication, 31,* 378–388.

Sommers, N. (1982). Responding to student writing. *College Composition and Communication, 33*(2), 148–156.

Spear, K. (1988). *Sharing writing: Peer response groups in English classes.* Portsmouth, NH: Boynton/Cook.

Speck, B. W. (1997). Respect for religious differences: The case of Muslim students. In D. L. Sigsbee, B. W. Speck, and B. Maylath (Eds.), *Approaches to teaching non-native English speakers across the curriculum* (pp. 39–46). New Directions for Teaching and Learning, no. 70. San Francisco: Jossey-Bass.

Speck, B. W. (1998a). *Grading student writing: An annotated bibliography.* Westport, CT: Greenwood Press.

Speck, B. W. (1998b). The teacher's role in the pluralistic classroom. *Perspectives, 28*(1), 19–43.

Speck, B. W. (1998c). Unveiling some of the mystery of professional judgment in classroom assessment. In R. S. Anderson and B. W. Speck (Eds.), *Changing the way we grade student performance: Classroom assessment and the new learning paradigm* (pp. 17–31). New Directions for Teaching and Learning, no. 74. San Francisco: Jossey-Bass.

Speck, B. W. (2000). *Grading students' classroom writing: Issues and strategies.* ASHE-ERIC Higher Education Report (vol. 27, no. 3). Washington, DC: Graduate School of Education and Human Development, The George Washington University.

Speck, B. W., Johnson, T. R., Dice, C. P., and Heaton, L. B. (1999). *Collaborative writing: An annotated bibliography.* Westport, CT: Greenwood Press.

Speck, B. W., and Jones, T. R. (1998). Direction in the grading of writing? What the literature on the grading of writing does and doesn't tell us. In F. Zak and C. C. Weaver (Eds.), *The theory and practice of grading writing: Problems and possibilities* (pp. 17–29). Albany: State University of New York Press.

Sperling, M. (1996). Revisiting the writing-speaking connection: Challenges for research on writing and writing instruction. *Review of Educational Research, 66*(1), 51–86.

Spiegelhalder, G. (1983). From darkness into light: A group process approach to the research paper. *Arizona English Bulletin, 26*(1), 91–106.

Spilka, R. (1993a). Collaboration across multiple organizational cultures. *Technical Communication Quarterly, 2*(2), 125–145.

Spilka, R. (Ed.). (1993b). *Writing in the workplace: New research perspectives.* Carbondale: Southern Illinois University Press.

Sproull, L., and Kiesler, S. (1986). Reducing social context cues: Electronic mail in organizational communication. *Management Science, 32*(11), 1492–1512.

Stage, F. K., Muller, P. A., Kinzie, J., and Simmons, A. (1998). *Creating learning centered classrooms: What does learning theory have to say?* ASHE-ERIC Higher Education Report (vol. 26, no. 4). Washington, DC: Graduate School of Education and Human Development, The George Washington University.

Stanley, L. C., and Ambron, J. (Eds.). (1991). *Writing across the curriculum in community colleges.* New Directions for Community Colleges, no. 73. San Francisco: Jossey-Bass.

Steffens, H. (1989). Collaborative learning in a history seminar. *History Teacher, 22*(2), 125–138.

Stewart, D. C. (1975). Aesthetic distance and the composition teacher. *College Composition and Communication, 26*(3), 238–243.

Stillinger, J. (1991). *Multiple authorship and the myth of solitary genius.* New York: Oxford University Press.

Sudol, R. A. (Ed.). (1982). *Revising: New essays for teachers of writing.* Urbana, IL: National Council of Teachers of English.

Sudol, R. A. (1985). Applied word processing: Notes on authority, responsibility, and revision in a workshop model. *College Composition and Communication, 36*(3), 331–335.

Sullivan, P. (1991). Collaboration between organizations: Contributions outsiders can make to negotiation and cooperation during composition. *Technical Communication, 38*(4), 485–492.

Sullivan, P. (1994). Computer technology and collaborative learning. In K. Bosworth and S. J. Hamilton (Eds.), *Collaborative learning: Underlying processes and effective techniques* (Vol. 59, pp. 59–67). San Francisco: Jossey-Bass.

Summers, T. F., and Redmen, D. L. (1989). Problems encountered while group writing: The students' point of view. In R. Louth and A. M. Scott (Eds.), *Collaborative technical writing: Theory and practice* (pp. 95–100). Hammond, LA: Association of Teachers of Technical Writing.

Tebeaux, E. (1991). The shared-document collaborative case response: Teaching and research implications of an in-house teaching strategy. In M. M. Lay and W. M. Karis (Eds.), *Collaborative writing in industry: Investigations in theory and practice* (pp. 124–145). Amityville, NY: Baywood.

Throckmorton, H. J. (1980, November). Do your writing assignments work? Checklist for a good writing assignment. *English Journal, 69,* 56–59.

Tirrell, M. K. (1981, Fall). The writing conference and the composing process. *The Writing Instructor, 1,* 7–14.

Tomlinson, S. (1990). Writing to learn: Back to another basic. In M. D. Svinicki (Ed.), *The changing face of college teaching* (pp. 31–39). New Directions for Teaching and Learning, no. 42. San Francisco: Jossey-Bass.

Tritt, M. (1983). Exchange grading with a workshop approach to the teaching of writing. *English Quarterly, 16*(1), 16–19.

Trzyna, T., and Batschelet, M. (1990). The ethical complexity of collaboration. *Writing on the Edge, 2*(1), 23–33.

Van Pelt, W., and Gillam, A. (1991). Peer collaboration and the computer-assisted classroom. In M. M. Lay and W. M. Karis (Eds.), *Collaborative writing in industry: Investigations in theory and practice* (pp. 170–206). Amityville, NY: Baywood.

Verner, C., and Dickinson, G. (1967). The lecture: An analysis and review of research. *Adult Education, 17,* 85–100.

Wachholz, P. (1996, October). What if they don't all understand English? Diversity in the peer-response group. *Tennessee English Journal, 7,* 41–44.

Waldrep, T. (Ed.). (1985). *Writers on writing* (3 vols.) New York: Random House.

Wall, S. V., and Hull, G. A. (1989). The semantics of error: What do teachers know? In C. M. Anson (Ed.), *Writing and response: Theory, practice, and research* (pp. 261–292). Urbana, IL: National Council of Teachers of English.

Walvoord, B.E.F. (1986). Student response groups: Training for autonomy. *The Writing Instructor, 6*(1), 39–47.

Watson-Roulin, V., and Peck, J. M. (1985). Double time. *Writer's Digest, 65*(3), 32–34, 36.

Whipple, W. R. (1987, October). Collaborative learning: Recognizing it when we see it. *AAHE Bulletin, 40,* 3–6.

White, E. M. (1995). *Assigning, responding, evaluating: A writing teacher's guide* (3rd ed.). New York: St. Martin's Press.

Williams, J. M. (1981). The phenomenology of error. *College Composition and Communication, 32*(2), 152–168.

Wilson, R. C. (1986). Improving faculty teaching: Effective use of student evaluations and consultants. *Journal of Higher Education, 57*(2), 196–211.

Yagelski, R. P. (1994). Collaboration and children's writing: What "real" authors do, what children do. *Journal of Teaching Writing, 12*(2), 217–233.

Yeoman, E. (1995). "Sam's café": A case study of computer conferencing as a medium for collective journal writing. *Canadian Journal of Educational Communication, 24*(3), 209–225.

Young, D. (1994). *The rhetoric of extremity: Teaching Adrienne Rich to undergraduates.* Paper presented at the annual meeting of the Conference on College Composition and Communication, Nashville, TN. (ED 372 388)

Zinsser, W. (1988). *Writing to learn.* New York: Harper & Row.

Zoellner, R. (1969). Talk-write: A behavioral pedagogy for composition. *College English, 30,* 267–320.

Name Index

Subject Index

ASHE-ERIC
Higher Education Reports

The mission of the Educational Resources Information Center (ERIC) system is to improve American education by increasing and facilitating the use of educational research and information on practice in the activities of learning, teaching, educational decision making, and research, wherever and whenever these activities take place.

Since 1983, the ASHE-ERIC Higher Education Report series has been published in cooperation with the Association for the Study of Higher Education (ASHE). Starting in 2000, the series has been published by Jossey-Bass in conjunction with the ERIC Clearinghouse on Higher Education.

Each monograph is the definitive analysis of a tough higher education problem, based on thorough research of pertinent literature and institutional experiences. Topics are identified by a national survey. Noted practitioners and scholars are then commissioned to write the reports, with experts providing critical reviews of each manuscript before publication.

Six monographs in the series are published each year and are available on individual and subscription bases. To order, use the order form at the back of this issue.

Qualified persons interested in writing a monograph for the series are invited to submit a proposal to the National Advisory Board. As the preeminent literature review and issue analysis series in higher education, the Higher Education Reports are guaranteed wide dissemination and provide national exposure for accepted candidates. Execution of a monograph requires at least a minimal familiarity with the ERIC database, including *Resources in Education* and the current *Index to Journals in Education*. The objective of these reports is to bridge conventional wisdom and practical research.

Advisory Board

Susan Frost
Office of Institutional Planning
and Research
Emory University

Kenneth Feldman
SUNY at Stony Brook

Anna Ortiz
Michigan State University

James Fairweather
Michigan State University

Lori White
Stanford University

Esther E. Gottlieb
West Virginia University

Carol Colbeck
Pennsylvania State University

Jeni Hart
University of Arizona

Review Panelists and Consulting Editors

Rick Abel
Stephen F. Austin State University

Becky Anderson
The University of Memphis

John A. Centra
Syracuse University

Carol L. Colbeck
Pennsylvania State University

Elizabeth A. Jones
West Virginia University

James C. Palmer
Illinois State University

Mary Ellen Pitts
Rhodes College

David L. Sigsbee
The University of Memphis

Recent Titles

Volume 28 ASHE-ERIC Higher Education Reports

1. The Changing Nature of the Academic Deanship
   Mimi Wolverton, Walter H. Gmelch, Joni Montez, and Charles T. Nies

2. Faculty Compensation Systems: Impact on the Quality of Higher Education
   Terry P. Sutton, Peter J. Bergerson

3. Socialization of Graduate and Professional Students in Higher Education:
   A Perilous Passage?
   John C. Weidman, Darla J. Twale, Elizabeth Leahy Stein

4. Understanding and Facilitating Organizational Change in the 21st Century: Recent
   Research and Conceptualizations
   Adrianna J. Kezar

5. Cost Containment in Higher Education: Issues and Recommendations
   Walter A. Brown, Cayo Gamber

Volume 27 ASHE-ERIC Higher Education Reports

1. The Art and Science of Classroom Assessment: The Missing Part of Pedagogy
   Susan M. Brookhart

2. Due Process and Higher Education: A Systemic Approach to Fair Decision Making
   Ed Stevens

3. Grading Students' Classroom Writing: Issues and Strategies
   Bruce W. Speck

4. Posttenure Faculty Development: Building a System for Faculty Improvement
   and Appreciation
   Jeffrey W. Alstete

5. Digital Dilemma: Issues of Access, Cost, and Quality in Media-Enhanced and Distance
   Education
   Gerald C. Van Dusen

6. Women and Minority Faculty in the Academic Workplace: Recruitment, Retention, and
   Academic Culture
   Adalberto Aguirre, Jr.

7. Higher Education Outside of the Academy
   Jeffrey A. Cantor

8. Academic Departments: How They Work, How They Change
   *Barbara E. Walvoord, Anna K. Carey, Hoke L. Smith, Suzanne W. Soled,
   Philip K. Way, Debbie Zorn*

Back Issue/Subscription Order Form

Copy or detach and send to:
Jossey-Bass, 989 Market Street, San Francisco, CA 94103-1741

Call or fax toll free!
Phone 888-378-2537 6AM-5PM PST; Fax 888-481-2665

Individual reports:	Please send me the following reports at $24 each
	(Important: please include series initials and issue number, such as AEHE 27:1)

1. AEHE _____

_____

_____

$ _____ Total for individual reports

$ _____ SHIPPING CHARGES: SURFACE

	Domestic	Canadian
First Item	$5.00	$6.50
Each Add'l Item	$3.00	$3.00

For next-day and second-day delivery rates, call the number listed above.

Subscriptions — Please ❏ start my subscription to *ASHE-ERIC Higher Education Reports* at the following rate (6 issues):
U.S.: $130   Canada: $130   All others: $178

$ _____ Total individual reports and subscriptions (Add appropriate sales tax for your state for individual reports. No sales tax on U.S. subscriptions. Canadian residents, add GST for subscriptions and individual reports.)

Federal Tax ID 135593032   GST 89102-8052

❏ Payment enclosed (U.S. check or money order only)

❏ VISA, MC, AmEx, Discover Card # _____ Exp. date _____

Signature _____ Day phone _____

❏ Bill me (U.S. institutional orders only. Purchase order required.)

Purchase order #_____

Name _____

Address _____

_____

Phone_____ E-mail _____

For more information about Jossey-Bass, visit our Web site at:
www.josseybass.com   **PRIORITY CODE = ND1**

Bruce W. Speck is professor of English and vice president for academic affairs at Austin Peay State University in Clarksville, Tennessee. Previously, he held positions at the University of North Carolina at Pembroke and at the University of Memphis. During his tenure at Memphis, he also was coordinator of the Writing-Across-the-Curriculum program for six years. His work has appeared in a variety of professional journals, including *Teaching and Teacher Education, Perspectives, Issues in Writing, College Student Journal, Technical Communication Quarterly,* and *Training and Development Journal.* He is coeditor of four volumes in the Jossey-Bass New Directions for Teaching and Learning Series and two volumes in the Jossey-Bass New Directions for Higher Education Series; he also published *Grading Student Writing: An Annotated Bibliography* for Greenwood Press and is author of *Grading Students' Classroom Writing: Issues and Strategies* in the ASHE-ERIC Higher Education Report Series.